Early Virginia Marriages

Virginia
County Records

VOLUME IV

EARLY VIRGINIA MARRIAGES

EDITED BY

William Armstrong Crozier

With a New Index by
Miss Anna M. Cartlidge

Originally published as Volume IV of *Virginia County Records*
New York, 1907
Reprinted: Southern Book Company
Baltimore, 1953
Reissued: Genealogical Publishing Company
Baltimore, 1968
Reissued (with a new Index): Genealogical Publishing Company
3600 Clipper Mill Rd., Suite 260
Baltimore, Maryland 21211-1953
1973, 1982, 1986, 2009
Library of Congress Catalogue Card Number 67-29835
ISBN 978-0-8063-0568-4
Made in the United States of America

Preface

THE Virginia marriage records are divided into two classes—those contained in the parish registers, and the marriage bonds or intentions, which were filed with the county clerk. The present volume treats principally with the latter class of records. It is, however, the Editor's intention to incorporate in future volumes, the marriage entries contained in hitherto unprinted parish registers, and already abstracts from two important old registers are nearly completed. ❡ As the marriage records are printed under their individual counties, it has not been deemed necessary to issue an index to this volume, but a small amount of time being necessary to consult the pages pertaining to the county in which the searcher is interested. A separate index volume will be issued upon the completion of the "Marriage Series."

The following table gives the date of the formation of the counties named in this volume.

Amelia, formed in 1734 from Prince George and Brunswick.

Augusta, formed in 1738 from Orange.

Charles City, one of the eight original shires of 1634.

Elizabeth City, one of the eight original shires of 1634.

Fauquier, formed in 1759 from Prince William.

King George, formed in 1720 from Richmond.

Lancaster, formed in 1652.

Lunenburg, formed in 1746 from Brunswick.

Middlesex, formed in 1673 from Lancaster.

Rockbridge, formed in 1777 from Augusta and Botetourt.

Southampton, formed in 1748 from Isle of Wight.

Surry, formed in 1652 from Isle of Wight.

Sussex, formed in 1754 from Surry.

Westmoreland, formed in 1652 from Northumberland.

York, one of the eight original shires of 1634.

Contents

Fauquier County

December 19, 1759,	Chandler Fowke and Mary Harrison
June 18, 1759,	Robert Wickliffe and Mary Hardin
November 30, 1759,	Joseph Hudnall and Mary Taylor
November 30, 1759,	Nimrod Ashby and Frances Wright
August 27, 1759,	Thomas Wood and Sarah Buchanan
˙December 19, 1760	Charles Chilton and Betty Blackwell
February 10, 1760,	George Wheatley and Diana Darnall
February 3, 1761,	William Moffett and Ann Stone
October 19, 1761,	Felix, Gilbert and Ann Grant
December 8, 1763,	James Wright and Mary Duncan
August 26, 1763,	Wm. Foote and Elizabeth Foote
September 22, 1763,	William Elliot and Eleanor Burger
August 21, 1764,	Rodham Tullos and Ann Finnie
December 6 1764,	William Allen and Mary Bradford
November 13, 1764,	Thos. Auberry and Ann Fletcher
May 31, 1764,	Martin Pickett and Ann Blackwell
April 9, 1764,	Benj. Tyler and Mary Foote
April 2, 1764,	Francis Moore and Frances Foote
December 24, 1764,	Wm. Jennings and Elizabeth Withers
February 23, 1764,	Wm. Helm and Lettice Neavil
December 26, 1764,	Charles Hume and Hannah Jones
October 29, 1764,	Benj. Hawkins and Ann Bowen
June 7, 1764,	John Claytor and Elizabeth Herrill
March 16, 1764,	William Edmonds and Elizabeth Blackwell
January 17, 1764,	James Peters and Winifred Ashby
December 30, 1764,	Benj. Bradford and Ann Allen
February 6, 1764,	William Seaton and Mary Kenner
November 16, 1764,	Richard Rixey and Elizabeth Morehead
February 11, 1765,	James Neflson and Betty Obanon
January 14, 1765,	William Tippet and Sarah Hill
July 23, 1765,	Henry Mauzy and Elizabeth Morgan
February 13, 1765,	Moses Green and Mary Blackwell
January 26, 1765,	Joseph Cockerel and Elizabeth Boaden

April 23, 1765,	Edmund Homes and Sarah Ann Starke
January 20, 1765,	Hezekiah Rhodes and Elizabeth Putnam
June 5, 1765,	Peter Rout and Ann Crosby
June 19, 1765,	Richard Boyce and Sarah Helm
October 17, 1765,	Minor Winn and Betty Withers
December, 11, 1766,	Benjamin Pope and Bahethelon Foote
January 15, 1766,	John Nelson and Mary Young
March 3, 1766,	James Blackwell and Ann Blackwell
July 18, 1766,	Ambrose Barnet and Judith Neavil
February 23, 1766,	William Harrison and Jane Hume
April 24, 1766,	John Foley and Milley Ashby
August 24, 1766,	John Wake and Mary Grigsby
April 27, 1766,	Wm. Hansborough and Sarah Watts
May 2, 1766,	Richard Jackman and Mary Neavil
April 24, 1766,	William Ashby and Mary Tibbs
March 3, 1766,	James Winn and Hannah Withers
February 18, 1766,	Joseph Duncan and Sarah Fletcher
February 23, 1764,	William Nash and Mary Bradford
October 25, 1768	Francis Atwell and Mary McDonald
November 22, 1768,	Samuel Moore and Eliz. McTeavor
December 12, 1768,	Josiah Fishback and Ann Nelson
October 21, 1768,	John Seaton and Alice Murry
November 10, 1768,	John Rhodes and Nancy Dutman
October 24, 1768,	Thomas Nelson and Rachael Grigsby
March 16, 1769,	William Withers and Hannah Rosser
February 2, 1769,	Joseph Barbee and Ann Withers
January 13, 1769,	Edward Huneston and Susannah Quarles
June 26, 1769,	Thomas Smith and Elizabeth Adams
June 9, 1769,	George Adams and Anna Turner
December 17, 1770,	George Davis and Elizabeth Grinan
November 20, 1770,	James Markham and Catherine Kenner
December 17, 1770,	William Butler and Margaret Jones
January 5, 1771,	Richard Head and Sarah Newport
August 20, 1771,	Nicholas Springs and Catherine Butcher
January 28, 1771,	Isaac McCoy and Bridget Withers
November 25, 1771,	Matthew Smith and Martha Winn
August 21, 1771,	Joseph Duncan and Hannah Freeman
May 28, 1771,	Peter Hord and Honor Wheatley
April 16, 1771,	Kimber Barton and Elizabeth Lewis
April 22, 1771,	James Ireland and Jane Burgess
September 5, 1771,	Samuel Arnold and Elizabeth Wright

October 18, 1771,	William Russell and Mary Darnall
June 14, 1771,	James Hackley and Mary Freeman
February 13, 1771,	Sanford Carroll and Betty Bartlętt
February 8, 1771,	William Grigsby and Elizabeth Bullitt
October 23, 1771,	Isaac Arnold and Mary Porter
December 23, 1771,	Joseph Nelson and Catherine O'Banon
March 25, 1771,	James Hathaway and Joanna Neavill
September 17, 1771,	George Hinson and Susanna Little
January 20, 1771,	John Rust and Elinor Atchison
February 18, 1771,	Jacob Fishback and Phebe Morgan
June 17, 1771,	John Fishback and Alice Morgan
December 21, 1771,	John Mitchell and Mary Rosser
October 13, 1772,	Robert Layton and Ann Stamp
July 22, 1772,	James Slaughter and Elizabeth Hampton
September 28, 1772,	Edward Settle and Rosanna Morgan
June 19, 1772,	Edward Walpole and Ann Chinn
March 9, 1772,	Charles Waller and Mary Crosby
March 12, 1772,	George Grant and Mary Shackleford
June 15, 1772,	Owen Campbell and Betty Little
June 29, 1772,	George Cloke and Alice Hudnall
March 21, 1772,	William Drummond and Winny Williams
July 31, 1772,	Thomas Neavil and Mary Stewart
February 27, 1772,	Richard Buckner and Judith Edmonds
June 27, 1772,	Henry Allen and Betty Nelson
November 26, 1772,	John Baxter and Amelia Briant
December 26, 1772,	Willy Roy and Sarah Fowkes
December 23, 1772,	Thomas Massey and Molley Morehead
August 23, 1773,	Tyler Waugh and Mary Crump
September 24, 1773,	William Stanton and Lucy Blackwell
July 19, 1773,	John Pope Williams and Hannah Minter
August 25, 1773,	Samuel Pearle and Dorcas Kerr
March 29, 1773,	Michael Robinson and Molly James
November 19, 1773,	James Withers and Sarah Pickett
January 2, 1774,	Charles Chaduck and Winifred Hainey
December 14, 1774,	William Hampton and Fanny Hunton
December 27, 1774,	Ephraim Hubbard and Ann Edmonds
October 24, 1774,	Frederick Kamper and Molly Jeffries
November 20, 1774,	Francis Morgan and Mary Read
December 20, 1774,	Francis Ash and Ann Adams
November 26, 1774,	Joseph Morgan and Elizabeth Bradford
June 16, 1774,	George Harris and Catherine Harris

April 2, 1774,	Michael Myers and Margaret Thornbury
June 7, 1774,	William Phillips and Elizabeth Fowke
May 22, 1775,	Josiah Basye and Sarah Sinclair
May 23, 1775,	Thomas Keith and Judith Blackwell
April 1, 1775,	Benjamin Berryman and Anna Bryant
November 4, 1775,	James Withers and Cloe Jennings
August 3, 1775,	Richard Price and Peggy James
May 13,1775,	William Green and Lucy Blackwell
February 2, 1775,	John Shumate and Susannah Crump
July 26, 1775,	Zeky Renoe and Mary Chinn
February 12, 1776,	John Carthroe and Molly Boswell
April 22, 1777,	John Smith and Mary Berryman
December 3, 1777,	Nathaniel Ashby and Peggy Mauzy
October 10, 1777,	Andrew O'Bannon and Mary Smith
September 22, 1777,	Robert Singleton and Drusilla Webb
July 28, 1777,	Patrick Whalon and Susannah Leach
July 10, 1777,	George Williams and Susannah Graham
October 16, 1777,	Francis Watts and Sarah Toby
March 17, 1777,	William Withers and Elizabeth Barber
December 20, 1777,	Joseph Neavil and Mary Elliot
June 3, 1777,	Joseph James and Mary James
August 11, 1777,	Samuel Jackson and Vashti Grinan
June 15, 1777,	William Freeman and Sallie Settle (or Little?)
March 24, 1777,	John Dulin and Fanny Glascock
August 28, 1777,	James Freeman and Elizabeth Sharpe
January 22, 1777,	John Catlett and Rachael Routt
May 9, 1777,	—— Berry and Susannah Feagan
May 7, 1777,	William Berry and Clara Feagan
August 9, 1777,	Joseph Bailey and Hannah Newby
January 2, 1777,	Thomas Bartlett and Sarah Carroll
May 20, 1777,	Battaley Bryan and Elizabeth Berryman
August 13, 1777,	Samuel Boyd and Molley Brooke
May 17, 1777,	George Berry and Sarah Conway
July 28, 1777,	Allen Redd and Susannah Bullett
March 31, 1777,	William Gibson and Hannah Settle
October 14, 1780,	Spencer Morgan and Susannah Kennen
May 30, 1780,	John Fletcher and Elizabeth Freeman
December 10, 1780,	John Nelson and Bathsheba Hogan
May 22, 1780,	William Baylis and Elizabeth Turner
May 23, 1780,	John Brian and Mary Linn
December 14, 1780,	Isaac Eustace and Susannah James

May 22, 1780,	Richard Lee and Ann Darnall
April 24, 1780,	Charles Rialls (or Ralls) and Hannah Brown
October 31, 1780,	John Hagan and Molly Mauzy
December 14, 1780,	William Jones and Ann Eustace
November 29, 1780,	John Bartlett and Ann Bartlett
December 30, 1780,	Augustin Smith and Susannah Darnall
November 27, 1780,	Elisha Harris and Margaret McCormick
November 13, 1780,	Benjamin O'Banon and Eleanor Ash
May 6, 1780,	John Dean and Elizabeth Praye
May 26, 1780,	William McLeod and Jane Bowmer
March 14, 1780,	George Asbury and Mary Taylor
May 13, 1780,	Jeduthon Blackerby and Mary Chamberlayne
May 16, 1780,	William Duncan and Lydia Duncan
December 1, 1780,	Samuel Blackwell and Peggy Gillison
November 15, 1780,	Benjamin Utterback and Elizabeth Snelling
December 4, 1780,	John Carter and Mary Wood
November 24, 1780,	Joshua King and Rachael Kennedy
September 26, 1781,	Thomas Blackwell and Judith Grant
November 26, 1781,	James Dobie and Ann Whitley
January 2, 1781,	Benjamin Payne and Susannah Roussan
December 17, 1781,	James Bowen and Rachael Bower
December 11, 1781,	Thomas Bowen and Sally Winterton
February 17, 1781,	Thomas Fitzhugh and Charlotte Moffett
May 25, 1781,	Matthew Carnor and Ann Hinson
July 30, 1781,	Joseph Silmon and Elender Truman
September 24, 1781,	John Murphew and Joan Waddell
January 10, 1781,	Jesse Kendall and Catherine Eastham
April 24, 1781,	John Ridley and Elizabeth Bailey
December 14, 1781,	Henry Allen and Catherine McKonkey
September 6, 1781,	Duncan Graham and Dolly Tarrow
January 18, 1781,	Charles Metcalf and Elizabeth Blackerby
August 4, 1781,	William Allen and Hannah Peppin
April 19, 1781,	Stephen Bailey and Susannah Luntsford
January 1, 1781,	Charles Morgan and Mary Robinson
May 22, 1781,	Robert McMekin and Patty Russell
October 19, 1781,	Nathaniel Pettit and Rebecca Owens
February 12, 1781,	Elijah Horton and Catherine Nelson
February 26, 1781,	John Vowles and Hannah Battaley
February 13, 1781,	Thomas Dowdall and Betty Wickliffe
May 16, 1781,	James Childs and Milley McKonkey
April 4, 1781,	John Simpson and Ann Bare

VIRGINIA MARRIAGES

April 13, 1781, George Bailey and Phebe Bragg
December 4, 1781, Richard Basye and Nancy Taylor
August 4, 1781, Hugh Bradley and Celia Basham
December 3, 1781, John Brown and Dolly Stringfellow
May 15, 1781, Charles Benson and Franky Benson
October 9, 1781, James Shirley and Mary McMekin
December 4, 1781, Simon Bailey and Hester Lunce
January 3, 1781, John Edge, Jr., and Nancy Cummins
August 2, 1781, Benjamin Ashby and Jane Ash
February 27, 1781, Peter Bruin and Elizabeth Edmonds
July 20, 1781, John Praye and Elizabeth Kirke
May 4, 1782, Edward Shacklett and Betsy Rector
August 26, 1782, Samuel Singleton and Mary Ann Connelly
March 25, 1782, John Norris and Mary Jones
August 5, 1782, Jacob Button and Sarah Kamper
October 28, 1782, David Wickliffe and Margaret Seaton
June 24, 1782, John Barbee and Margry Dyson
January 16, 1782, Wharton Ransdell and Mary Morehead
September 9, 1782, Philip Spitler, Jr., and Elizabeth Hume
January 28, 1782, James Green and Elizabeth Jones
June 10, 1782, Strother Settle and Dorothy Ash
June 17, 1782, Stephen Donaldson and Susanna Boswell
December 21, 1782, John Wilkinson and Lucretia Moffett
May 8, 1782, Thomas Gibson and Charlotte Beale
September 30, 1782, John Cannon and Sarah Harrison Brazier
April 18, 1782, William Smith and Ann Ashby
June 12, 1782, John Turner and Jenny Bailey
September 18, 1782, Nathaniel Weedon and Mary Smith
October 31, 1782, Benjamin Morgan and Elizabeth Kemper
September 23, 1782, Francis Brown and Elizabeth Smith
March 26, 1782, James Freeman and Margaret Williams
October 28, 1782, George Williams and Ann Sharp
June 8, 1782, Jesse Maddux and Judith Blackerby
May 1, 1782, John Metcalf and Milly Shackelford
September 13, 1782, John Gillison and Sarah Alexander
September 2, 1782, Joseph Obanon and Elizabeth Grigsby
November 14, 1782, George Hampton and Mary Nugent Ballard
December 31, 1782, Thomas Porter and Susanna Porter
February 11, 1782, William Bagley and Nancy Newby
February 11, 1782, Marquis Calmes, Jr., and Priscilla Heale
May 1, 1782, Samuel Moore and Lucy Payne

April 8, 1782,	Nathaniel Holtzclaw and Isa Gibson
October 12, 1782,	John Morgan and Anna Thomas
October 28, 1782,	Alexander Linn and Hannah Kamper
February 13, 1782,	Eli Davis and Frances Bannister
February 12, 1782,	John Hopper and Jane McMekin
November 24, 1783,	Philip Mallory and Jane Harrison
February 24, 1783,	Benjamin Withers and Nanny Robinson
May 26, 1783,	Cuthbert Peyton and Catherine Bronaugh
January 7, 1783,	John White and Ann Bailey
November 15, 1783,	Isachar Paulin and Rachael Bryan
April 28, 1783,	Robert Ashby and Catherine Combs
March 18, 1783,	John Turley and Susanna Squires
March 17, 1783,	Martin Edwards and Celia Garner
December 1, 1783,	Samuel Wharton and Rebecca Bowner
October 20, 1783,	John Peters and Ann Roussan
October 31, 1783,	Benjamin Roberson and Margt. Bruce James
September 22, 1783,	Gabriel Green and Sarah Ann Grant
April 28, 1783,	Joseph Barbee and Elizabeth Laurance
November 24, 1783,	Peter Glascock and Anna Glascock
December 31, 1783,	John Cooke and Nancy Fielding
December 10, 1783,	Samuel Pettit and Elizabeth Bragg
October 1, 1783,	Benjamin Wigginton and Mary Thornberry
December 20, 1783,	Jesse Orear and Melinda Holton
July 20, 1783,	Henry Floyd and Franky Crosby
January 25, 1783,	William Fargerson and Dolly Amiss
January 21, 1783,	Thomas Obanon and Hannah Barker
January 20, 1783,	John Austin and Elizabeth Burges
March 24, 1783,	John Gibson, Jr., and Ann Eustace
September 11, 1783,	Thomas Marshall, Jr., and Susannah Adams
October 27, 1783,	John Ashby and Catherine Hufman
September 17, 1783,	William Coppage and Sarah Realey
March 4, 1783,	Uriel Ash and Milly Churchill
June 14, 1783,	James Healey and Lucy Jeffreis
January 14, 1784,	Ephraim Abell and Betsy Stringfellow
October 20, 1785,	John Ballard and Mary Brown
October 20, 1785,	Seymour Arnold and Molly Knowling
December 30, 1785,	Henry Bramlett and Gladah Gough
June 20, 1785,	Robert Bates and Betsy Johnson
April 20, 1785,	George Brooke and Judy Marshall
February 14, 1785,	William Laurence Buckley and Mary Ships
December 29, 1785,	Thomas Byrn and Elizabeth Leach

March 19, 1785,	William Brown and Mary Parker
October 20, 1785,	Thomas Brown and Ann Ash
March 23, 1785,	John Beatty and Nancy Shipp
May 29, 1786,	Robert Brown and Molly Boyd
May 11, 1785,	Zachariah Benson and Sarah Partlow
September 21, 1785,	William Blackmore and Betsy Bashaw
November 20, 1785,	John Boyd and Milly Wright
September 28, 1785,	Daniel Cummins and Sarah Sullivan
November 23, 1785,	Dale Conter and Molly Robinson
January 26, 1785,	Vincent Cooper and Mary Cooper
September 26, 1785,	William Day and Nelly Corder
September 9, 1785,	Joseph Duncan and Hannah Jennings
April 14, 1785,	John Dell and Sarah Maddux
December 22, 1785,	William Embrey and Frankey Duncan
June 1, 1785,	Reuben Field and Frances Jones
December 20, 1785,	Samuel Fisher and Mary Pinkard
March 13, 1785,	James Garrett and Anna McCoy
May 12, 1785,	John Green and Betty Collins
August 2, 1785,	Robert Garr and Alinder Cox
November 28, 1785,	Aaron Grigsby and Milly Moffett
October 24, 1785,	Aaron George and Lydia Robinson
February 15, 1785,	Taliaferro Grigsby and Elizabeth Keith
October 20, 1785,	Epaphroditus Hubbard and Ann McCarthy
Edmondson	
November 9, 1785,	Gilson Hamrick and Sally Thomas
April 13, 1785,	Gustavus Brown Horner and Frances Scott
December 10, 1785,	John Tinsal (or Linsal) and Sarah Button
December 12, 1785,	William Triplett and Elizabeth Morehead
September 20, 1785,	Anthony Hailey and Mary Dennison
May 28, 1785,	Allen Stewart and Sarah Grinan
July 10, 1785,	John Shaw and Fanny Cleveland
June 1, 1785,	Thomas Sanders and Molly Rogers
February 19, 1785,	Joshua Singleton and Nancy Withers Winn
December 30, 1785,	Benjamin Suthard and Ann Payne
September 26, 1785,	Delaney Smith and Mary Wright
November 8, 1785,	William Singleton and Susanna Floweree
February 20, 1785,	George Renoe and Jean Baylis
August 31, 1783,	Berryman Smith and Elizabeth Martin
September 20, 1785,	James Sherlock and Judy Norman
October 3, 1785,	Spencer Rector and Mary Tiffin
April 25, 1785,	Thomas Read and Milly Fishback

June 23, 1785,	Valentine Leach and Molly Furrow
July 16, 1785,	George Leach and Ann Craig
October 20, 1785,	John Knowling and Jemima Arnold
November 23, 1785,	William Kirkpatrick and Mary Feagan
February 11, 1785,	Robert Kenner and Dolly Clarke
December 15, 1785,	James Sparks and Margaret Dawson
April 16, 1785,	Thomas Pettit and Behethelon Owens
October 25, 1785,	John Underwood and Susanna Teagle
June 20, 1785,	Charles West and Sally Withers
September 5, 1785,	James Wood and Elizabeth Evans
September 3, 1785,	Arthur Harriss and Elizabeth Goff
March 16, 1785,	Benjamin Hardin and Nancy Routt
December 21, 1785,	Jacob Hayes and Bettie Rector
September 12, 1785,	Joseph Jeffries and Mary Young
June 27, 1785,	John James and Elizabeth Wright
September 19, 1783,	John Hailey and Peggy Jett
December 27, 1785,	George Leach and ——— Bigbie
March 13, 1786,	John Larrance and Joyce O'Bannon
December 21, 1785,	Benjamin Mahorney and Elizabeth Harriss
June 3, 1786,	David McClanahan and Elizabeth Fryer
August 22, 1785,	William Mott and Mary Welch
December 15, 1785,	David Maybin and Catherine Kenner
January 12, 1785,	William Mallony and Lucy Harrison
October 3, 1785,	Elijah Robinson and Susannah Norris
June 17, 1785,	John Porter and Jean Smith
August 24, 1785,	John Roach and Patty McClanahan
January 11, 1785,	James White and Mary Minter
October 2, 1785,	Joseph Shipp and Letty Etcheson
October 24, 1785,	George Martin and Elizabeth McCormack
July 25, 1785,	John Adams and Betsey McCormack
November 27, 1786,	William Owens and Nancy Owens
November 27, 1786,	Charles Duncan and Peggy Kish
October 23, 1786,	John Austin and Elizabeth Browning
August 1, 1786,	James Foley and Elizabeth Ogleby
September 24, 1786,	James Lamkin and Sarah Barker
September 26, 1786,	Nathaniel Gray and Sally Ransdell
July 13, 1786,	John Allen and Hannah Snelling
January 4, 1786,	William Alford and Fanny Suttle
March 8, 1786,	Francis Berryman and Elizabeth Barr
January 23, 1786,	William Barber and Ann Hickerson
February 28, 1786,	Thomas Bailey and Sarah Ball

January 7, 1786,	Isaac Basye and Frances Bashaw
December 20, 1786,	William Bradford and Molly Steel
November 17, 1786,	David Bragg and Margaret Crawley
November 5, 1786,	Daniel Boyd and Sarah Scroggin
March 11, 1786,	Austin Bradford and Elizabeth Hord
January 10, 1786,	William Courtney and Anna Smith
December 23, 1786,	Charles Christy and Nancy Smith
October 25, 1786,	John Coppage and Peggy Raley
January 11, 1786,	Elias Edmonds and Frances Edmonds
February 3, 1786,	Martin Dye and Haney Hinson
March 8, 1786,	Joshua Drumond and Mary Kidwell
October 30, 1786,	Daniel Donaldson and Cary Morehead
March 14, 1786,	Levi Davis and Lydia Kearns
January 11, 1786,	Nimrod Duncan and Hannah Martin
December 25, 1786,	George Einsor and Docia Stephens
August 25, 1786,	Francis Eviston and Celah Fletcher
April 4, 1786,	Jesse Embrey and Mary Hickerson
December, 25, 1786,	Robert Foster and Milley Leake
August 28, 1786,	George Foster and Sarah Conway
June 1, 1786,	Joseph George and Lydia Shumate
December 23, 1786,	Benj. Grigsby and Elizabeth Duncan
December 18, 1786,	Arthur Gladston and Susannah Hitt
September 4, 1786,	Samuel Grigsby and Franky Cornwell
October 18, 1786,	Gabriel George and Mary Neale
June 14, 1786,	George Graham and Alice Blackwell
March 14, 1786,	Simon Morgan and Elizabeth Pickett
September 26, 1786,	George Monroe and Mary Green
January 31, 1786,	George Glendenning and Milly Duncan
December 18, 1786,	William Green and Mary Ann Crockett
January 18, 1786,	James Hinson and Ann Quisenberry
January 3, 1786,	Archibald Holtzclaw and Miriam Hitt
July 11, 1786,	Davis Holden and Anna Shumate
	John Hand and Jenny Angle Robinson
January 11, 1786,	John Homes and Agatha Hume
December 23, 1786,	William Hailey and Nancy Jett
March 11, 1786,	James Hord and Sarah Hord
May 2, 1786,	Rawley Hogan and Peggy Conway
February 4, 1786,	Moses Jones and Sarah Hamilton
April 19, 1786,	Richard Jones and Sarah Guy
March 27, 1786,	John Jeffries and Alice Goodrich
December 30, 1786,	John Jones and Elizabeth Tibbetts

August 8, 1786,	William Lear and Hannah Bailey
August 21, 1786,	Wilfred Johnson and Mary Peyton
May 13, 1786,	Enoch Kim Withers and Jenny Chinn
October 4, 1786,	Lewis Jennings and Lucinda Bradford
November 1, 1786,	Thomas Jenkins and Katy Robinson
April 24, 1786,	Lawrence Triplett and Benedictine Triplett
May 17, 1786,	Alexander Turner and Peggy Rollins
June 22, 1786,	Paul Williams and Sarah Wheatley
September 16, 1786,	Benjamin West and Elizabeth Wren
December 6, 1786,	Alexander Wilson and Mary Oliver
October 31, 1786,	William Waddell and Ann White
March 28, 1786,	William Withers and Patty Ashby
July 31, 1786,	William Younglove and Elinor Carter
February 10, 1786,	Laban Shipp and Rebecca Turner
December 31, 1786,	James Jones and Mary Bradford
November 30, 1786,	Archibald Johnston and Jemima O'Banon
August 26, 1786,	Thomas Kerns and Mary Russell
March 11, 1786,	Abner Luttrell and Sarah Kelly
April 26, 1786,	Daniel Lowry and Ann Embrey
December 18, 1786,	Rodham Lundsford and Clement Ball
January 29, 1786,	Edward Lawrence and Nancy Priest
January 9, 1786,	Rodham Lawrence and Elizabeth Lawrence
December 18, 1786,	John McCoy and Uriah Hickman
December 26, 1786,	Samuel Meall and Elizabeth Luttrell
September 13, 1786,	William Moss and Lydia Glascock
March 25, 1786,	Colbert Mason and Margaret Rogers
June 19, 1786,	John McDaniel and Fenton Horton
November 21, 1786,	McClanahan Moore and Elizabeth Metcalf
July 18, 1786,	Daniel Marr and Susanna Jennings
October 30, 1786,	Charles Morehead and Margaret Slaughter
March 9, 1786,	Nathaniel Maddux and Anne Tennison
January 20, 1786,	Mason Priest and Sally Larrance
December 18, 1786,	James Neale and Sarah Pinckard
March 1, 1786,	Jesse Duncan and Rose Duncan
March 11, 1786,	Charles Porter and Anna Benson
December 21, 1786,	John Proctor and Elizabeth Hudnall
February 26, 1786,	William Richards and Ann Blackwell
November 18, 1786,	Thomas Ransdell and Mary Ransdell
March 25, 1786,	Aaron Roose and Ruth Phillips
April 23, 1786,	Fielding Scanland and Sophia Spiller
December 18, 1786,	Nimrod Stone and Sarah Russell

August 4, 1786,	Cadwallader Slaughter and Mary Fowke
February 15, 1786,	Jordan Little and Lucy Crafford
May 23, 1786,	George Seaton and Sarah Seaton
June 13, 1786,	William Settle and Sallie Garner
August 10, 1786,	Samuel Stephenson and Barbara Hagar
September 11, 1787,	Charles Marshall and Lucy Pickett
March 22, 1787,	John Allen and Seley Hefflin
April 17, 1787,	Joshua Athey and Elizabeth Hitch
August 14, 1787,	William Broadhurst and Frankey Harrill
June 25, 1787,	Daniel Bishop and Ann Leake
August 7, 1787,	Greenberry Barry and Frances Terry Davis
September 14, 1787,	John Bradford and Sally Barbee
November 29, 1787,	Edward Burgess and Frances Porter
December 21, 1787,	Henry Colvin and Catherine Williams
May 26, 1787,	Ambrose Gaunt and Sarah Vaughan
August 15, 1787,	Robert Green and Frances Edmonds
January 3, 1787,	James Carter and Sarah Dermont
September 24, 1787,	James Callahan and Elizabeth Phillips
January 8, 1787,	John Dunford and Elizabeth Folks
February 21, 1787,	William Dermont and Mary Williams
March 21, 1787,	Henry Dennison and Jenny Dixon
December 18, 1787,	William Darnall and Elizabeth Monroe
March 10, 1787,	Benjamin Eady and Margaret Gibson Gillison
October 16, 1787,	Hugh Goddard and Mary Avis
February 28, 1787,	James Green and Celid Triplett
December 17, 1787,	Nimrod Grimsley and Amelia Roberts
October 9, 1787,	Archibald Glasscock and Hannah Kincheloe
October 15, 1787,	Henry Harriss and Joanna Williams
April 7, 1787,	Isaac Harper and Jemima Constable
November 28, 1787,	Jesse Hinson and Elizabeth Cranford
February 27, 1787,	John Hitch and Cassandra Elgin
April 19, 1787,	Jesse Hinson and Mary Sullivan
April 9, 1787,	Joseph Harrington and Mary Hathaway
December 24, 1787,	George Jeffries and Molly Glascock
January 3, 1787,	Isaac James and Sarah Parker
January 8, 1787,	John James and Lavisa Wood
December 29, 1787,	Dempsey Jackson and Molly Pickett
December 11, 1787,	Thomas James and Hannah White
February 9, 1787,	Thomas Groves and Amelia Williams
May 2, 1787,	John Kemper and Martha Fisher
November 26, 1787,	Rodham Kenner and Jemima Barker

July 4, 1787,	John Knight and Susanna Boscarver
December 5, 1787,	James Kittson and Mary Brown
March 25, 1787,	Price Key and Sallie McQueen
February 2, 1787,	James Lee and Mary Lee
March 3, 1787,	Moses Lacey and Henrietta Pratt
June 18, 1787,	John Lion and Susanna Holtzclaw
July 3, 1787,	George Embrey Loyd and Ann Brown
March 14, 1787,	Benjamin Murry and Elizabeth Grant
December 31, 1787,	Hazael Harrill and Caty Shanks
December 24, 1787,	Alexander Majors and Letty Howell
April 21, 1787,	William McCoy and Nancy Kendall
January 25, 1787,	James Monroe and Sally Willis
January 10, 1787,	Robert Matthews and Sally Rogers
March 9, 1787,	Joseph McCoy and Mary Williams
July 16, 1787,	Richard McCoy and Milly Elliott
December 12, 1787,	Cornelius McCarthy and Sukey Hardwick
August 7, 1787,	Enoch Murray and Frances Crosby
December 22, 1787,	Nimrod Martin and Fanny Hopwood
December 11, 1787,	William Nalls and Mary Bailey
December 17, 1787,	Bethel Owens and Elizabeth Owens
April 24, 1787,	Thomas O'Neal and Esther Murray
December 29, 1787,	Martin Parker and Mary Shumate
April 9, 1787,	Henry Powell and Sally Strother
November, 6, 1787,	Jehu Popkins and Sally Perry
September 8, 1787,	John Robertson and Elizabeth Benson
January 12, 1787,	William Russell and Mary Curtis
December 24, 1787,	John Smith and Rebecca Spicer
January 11, 1787,	John Singer and Peggy Crosby
February 5, 1787,	Joseph Slaughter and Rachel Harper
February 26, 1787,	William Shumate and Frances Norman
March 31, 1787,	Henry Stickle and Caty Michael
December 24, 1787,	William Stevenson and Sarah Hickman
May 11, 1787,	William Settle and Melinda Hunton
February 19, 1787,	John Wills and Susannah Smith
February 5, 1787,	William Threltgeld and Chloe Spiller
December, 31, 1787,	William Williams and Elizabeth Settle
October 29, 1787,	Elijah Willoughby and Mary Leachman
July 12, 1787,	Mark Wood and Mary Bashaw
August 21, 1787,	Ambrose Walden and Elizabeth Taylor
January 8, 1788,	Charles Adams and Nancy ———
April 14, 1788,	Lawrence Ashton and Elizabeth Scott

October 27, 1788,	Theophilus Anderson and Molly Lear
March 10, 1788,	Thomas Braughan and Elizabeth Wilson
January 8, 1788,	Thomas Bailey and Sarah Campbell
January 14, 1788,	Lunford Bennett and Anna Crimm
February 25, 1788,	Henry Bailir and Sophia Edmonds
October 7, 1788,	Joseph Broadhurst and Sally Faubin
February 4, 1788,	Alexander Brink and Elizabeth Sullivan
December 17, 1788,	William Burdett and Mary Churley
February 9, 1788,	William Ball and Ann Keas
April 8, 1788,	John Bales and Barbary Redd
October 13, 1788,	Green Bailey and Mary Bragg
October 11, 1788,	Achilles G. Barnett and Ann James
December 29, 1788,	Thomas Brown and Molly Sanders
October 17, 1788,	Robert Benson and Ann Stringfellow
December 1, 1788,	John Bland and Hannah Randall
December 27, 1788,	Samuel Blackwell and Mary Bragg
July 20, 1788,	Benjamin Carpenter and Elizabeth McFarlin
February 18, 1788,	Bailis Corder and Parisaid Stone
February 20, 1788,	William Clayton and Elizabeth Chinn
August 9, 1788,	William Connór and Frankey Greening
December 20, 1788,	John Crupper and Ann Thomas
July 2, 1788,	John Crosson and Acksa Lewis
March 24, 1788,	James Canard and Lettice Jeffries
July 7, 1788,	Joseph Conway and Sarah Turner
December 26, 1788,	William Colvin and Anna George
December 4, 1788,	David Cowhay and Susanna Maddux
January 7, 1788,	John Duff and Mary Whitney
February 15, 1788,	Christopher Duncan and Elizabeth Hilburn
January 21, 1788,	Brawner Dowdall and Alice Homes
January 28, 1788,	Edward Dulin and Elizabeth Rhodes
April 5, 1788,	Rawleigh Darnall and Winifred Brown
October 14, 1788,	James Emmons and Caty Stegler
September 22, 1788,	William Finnie and Lilly Collins
August 25, 1788,	Andrew Froggett and Mocin Smith
September 17, 1788,	Richard Fletcher and Elizabeth Ratcliffe
March 24, 1788,	William Gutridge and Susanna Fishback
December 1, 1788,	John Glascock and Ann Hathaway
May 5, 1788,	George Grazer and Elizabeth Riley
August 25, 1788,	Jesse Green and Elizabeth Nelson
December 2, 1788,	Micajah Glasscock and Catherine Rector
July 20, 1788,	John Hammons and Susanna Hefferling

February 9, 1788,	William Hopper and Letty Williams
February 19, 1788,	James Hill and Sarah Leach
September 6, 1788,	Steward Hatfield and Rebecca Fidler
October 27, 1788,	William Hancock and Susanna Grigsby
December 29, 1788,	Charles Horton and Elizabeth Cooper
December 20, 1788,	Rolly Holly and Mary Colvin
August 8, 1788,	Tunis Johnson and Rose Settle
September 29, 1788,	John Warner Jones and Mary Tullos
August 18, 1788,	Henry Jeffries and Mary Chamberlain
August 25, 1788,	Anderson Jeffries and Mary Gordon
April 5, 1788,	Thomas Kidwell and Elizabeth Pearson
May 3, 1788,	Britain Lewis and Ann Crupm
March 24, 1788,	Mason Lawrence and Nancy O'Banon
August 23, 1788,	Hancock Lee and Lina Ann Eustace
October 18, 1788,	Peter Kamper and Susannah Fisher
December 22, 1788,	Joshua Mitchell and Elizabeth Stiggers
December 29, 1788,	Elias Metcalf and Sally Pickett
January 22, 1788,	George Minon and Mildred Heale
February 12, 1788,	Jesse Mason and Nancy Embrey
June 7, 1788,	Joseph King and Mary Bethell
May 24, 1788,	Elisha Thomas and Alice Glascock
February 14, 1788,	Benjamin Thomas and Catherine Glascock
November 5, 1788,	Stephen Zolle and Ann Crosby
September 29, 1788,	William Welch and Lydia Congreve
February 15, 1788,	John McDaniel and Eve Climan
October 29, 1788,	Studley Middleton and Nancy Wickliffe
December 26, 1788,	Simon Matthew and Molly Stamps
November 25, 1788,	Richard Nutt and Elizabeth Hathaway
December 19, 1788,	Benjamin Northent and Winney Brooks
February 9, 1788,	John Young and Elizabeth Singleton
February 29, 1788,	James Thomas and Peggy Stevenson
February 25, 1788,	Moses Rector and Elizabeth Green
June 16, 1788,	Original Roe and Sarah Kenner
September 6, 1788,	Daniel Routh and Martha Stigler
June 11, 1788,	Edward Smoot and Susannah Hitch
January 28, 1788,	John Shumate and Sarah Preston
March 19, 1788,	Scarlett Smith and Lydia Jackson
October 24, 1788,	John Smith and Margaret Allen
July 28, 1789,	William Markham and Mary Smith
April 17, 1789,	James Martin and Aga Hughes
May 21, 1789,	Matthew Waddell and Elizabeth Waddell

October 29, 1789,	Daniel McLaren (or McClair) and Mary Dodd
January 10, 1789,	Joseph Nay and Frances Mahoney
December 1, 1789,	John Northent and Nancy Henry
February 23, 1789,	Nimrod Young and Elizabeth Settle
August 28, 1789,	Josias Oliver and Mary Morehead
May 30, 1789,	James Penny and Lydia Dulin
March 17, 1789,	Christian Porter and Elizabeth Baker
March 17, 1789,	William Payne, Jr., and Molly Ann Payne
December 21, 1789,	Valentine Peyton and Sally Hale
February 18, 1789,	Abraham Parker and Priscilla McKoy
March 16, 1789,	Martin Porter and Aggy Withers
January 14, 1789,	Augustine Payne and Caty Young
June 22, 1789,	John Roberts and Sally Holly
August 25, 1789,	George Roberts and Anna Foster
March 23, 1789,	Henry Rogers and Sally Jett
January 26, 1789,	Reuben Redding and Elizabeth Roberts
June 19, 1789,	Bailey Rice and Elizabeth Morehead
December 16, 1789,	John Smoot and Peggy Hitch
July 29, 1789,	William Smith and Elizabeth McQueen
October 23, 1789,	James Smith and Sally Dunemont
December 20, 1789,	Nathaniel Snape and Fanny Kidwell
April 14, 1789,	John Smith and Betsy Williams
November 21, 1789,	George Stukle and Jenny Michael
February 17, 1789,	John Shaver and Mary Neale
March 23, 1789,	William Tomlin and Lissy Rogers
November 30, 1789,	Benamin Taylor and Catherine Weavei
January 16, 1789,	William Thayer and Hannah Jones
April 29, 1789,	William Tracey and Winny Grigsby
April 3, 1789,	Annett Underwood and Elizabeth Teagle
September 7, 1789,	Charles Utterback and Jemima Nelson
August 6, 1789,	Jesse Withers and Catherine Porter
June 29, 1789,	Goring White and Leanna Duncan
February 9, 1789,	Rush Hictson (or Watson) and Ann Christy
January 15, 1789,	George Foard and Charity Colvert
August 28, 1789,	William Ferguson and Ann Piper
January 26, 1789,	James Garrett and Phebe Harley
January 20, 1789,	William Glascock and Ann Green
April 28, 1789,	Alexander Gibson and Lucy Jeffries
March 18, 1789,	Nathaniel Gray and Betsey Ransdell
November 23, 1789,	Samuel Harriss and Nancy Duncan
March 3, 1789,	John Hansbrough and Sarah Lehogan

May 29, 1789,	William Hall and Frances Kenard
December 17, 1789,	Pierce Bailey Henderson and Milly Duncan
March 25, 1789,	William Helm and Aga Pickett
March 11, 1789,	Thomas Heaton and Susannah Taylor
December 26, 1789,	Thomas Haney and Margaret Chappclear
August 24, 1789,	Burr Harrison and Lucy Pickett
October 27,	William Heflin and Tilly Collins
September 15, 1789,	John Hind and Celia Furr
April 29, 1789,	William Huffman and Ann Guy
June 18, 1789,	William Jacobs and Mary Boswell
June 23, 1789,	Robert Jones and Dolly Ashby
March 21, 1789,	David Johnson and Sarah Odor
January 26, 1789,	Lewis Kemper and Hannah Basye
December 23, 1789,	Andrew Kenny and Nancy Horton
June 4, 1789,	James Knowland and Elizabeth Embry
December 8, 1789,	Joseph Linn and Sarah Brooks
March 2, 1789,	John Lowe and Frankey Adams
June 27, 1789,	Henry Logan and Catherine Hening
January 28, 1789,	Benjamin McBee and Hannah Randall
February 2, 1789,	Joseph McCoy and Mildred Taylor
November 23, 1789,	William McClanahan and Elizabeth Tillery
February 11, 1789,	Leander Murphey and Rose Duncan
December 16, 1789,	John Miller and Nancy Hitt
September 14, 1789,	William Arrasmith and Susanna McBee
March 7, 1789,	John Bruin and Mary Wilson
December 10, 1789,	Winter Bailey and Ann Norris
February 26, 1789,	James Broadbent and Sarah Bailey
December 11, 1789,	James Bishop and Cloe Lake
December 26, 1789,	William Bronaugh and Jane Hale
December 21, 1789,	John Barker and Sarah Glasscock
April 1, 1789,	James Burton and Nancy Singer
January 12, 1789,	Joseph Barnett and Mary Hitt
November 19, 1789,	George Bowmer and Priscilla Duncan
March 20, 1789,	William Bailey and Betsey Minor
May 14, 1789,	Charles Barker and Jean Drake
August 6, 1789,	John William Blake and Mary Lane
October 7, 1789,	William Crawford and Susanna Holder
January 9, 1789,	Chichester Chinn and Susanna Withers
December 15, 1789,	Hugh Chinn and Peggy Ash
August 25, 1789,	Timothy Cunningham and Sarah Fishback
December 25, 1789,	Thomas Chinn and Ann Hendley Moor

December 21, 1789,	Nathan Cockran and Margaret Keys
January 5, 1789,	John Clarke and Mary Ransdell
March 5, 1789,	William Carter and Mary Chesher
December 22, 1789,	William Devers and Elizabeth Johnston
September 8, 1789,	Lewis Dulin and Ann Shud
January 21, 1789,	William Eustace and Mary Gillison
December 22, 1789,	William Ellis and Nancy Clendenninng
June 22, 1789,	Edward Feagan and Polly Sinkler
August 25, 1789,	George Roach and Sarah White
February 22, 1790,	Minor Johnson and Hannah Johnson
December 7, 1790,	James Kincheloe and Elizabeth Hardwick
May 25, 1790,	Henry Camack and Molly Ellis
March 22, 1789,	Joseph Darnall and Sarah Ball
May 17, 1789,	Thomas Dennaby and Ann Carter
September 24, 1789,	George Day and Susanna Dennis
August 23, 1789,	John Day and Nancy Hudnall
February 24, 1789,	Nimrod Johnson and Polly Adams
March 1, 1789,	James Foley and Mary Bradford
July 26, 1789,	John Farnin and Lettice Riley
August 28, 1789,	Andrew Foster and Jane Crouch
December 22, 1789,	Joseph Garner and Sally Oar
March 19, 1790,	Vincent Golding and Nancy Burditt
December 15, 1790,	Allen Guttridge and Lucy Deal
February 22, 1790,	Nimrod Ganett and Elizabeth McCoy
October 30, 1790,	Cornelius Anderson and Katy Riddle
March 4, 1790,	Gavin Adams and Susanna Miller
December 11, 1790,	Joseph Anderson and Charlotte Freeman
October 19, 1790,	Thomas Bronaugh and Peggy Kerr
February 23, 1790,	Thomas Burroughs and Lettice Kendall
December 29, 1790,	Dozier Bragg and Peggy Bussey
August 12, 1790,	James Bartlett and Sarah Phillips
November 22, 1790,	William Barnet and Catherine Smith
October 22, 1790,	Martin Covert and Susanna O'Bannon
December 16, 1790,	Henry Ford and Nancy Payne
October 23, 1790,	Peter Hansbrough and Ann Harrison
September 1, 1790,	George Herndon and Elizabeth Stephens
September 16, 1790,	William Hailey and Susanna Jett
April 21, 1790,	John Humphries and Dorothy McConchie
June 20, 1790,	John Hickman and Ann Thompson
October 19, 1790,	William Horner and Mary Edmonds
January 14, 1790,	Cornelius Head and Margaret Hilkins

August 9, 1790,	Charles Martin and Frankey Fishback
December 25, 1790,	Robert McConchie and Mary Ann King
June 12, 1790,	John Moring and Sarah Fishback
January 15, 1790,	Carwithy Magraw and Margaret Glasscock
November 15, 1790,	Martin McCloud and Nancy Folks
April 14, 1790,	Thomas Neale and Elizabeth Roizier
February 10, 1790,	Daniel McCoy and Agnes Kamper
April 5, 1790,	David Robinson and Sally Wilson
February 5, 1790,	Fielding Phillips and Nancy Linton
October 20, 1790,	Colston Payne and Charity Smoot
June 15, 1790,	Samuel Pearle and Nancy Strother
November 3, 1790,	James Patterson and Nancy Constable
June 7, 1790,	Jeremiah Preston and Molly Ellis
November 20, 1790,	John Pickett and Elizabeth Chamberlain
June 21, 1790,	Edward Rogers and Elizabeth Hathaway
January 19, 1790,	Charles Shaw and Catherine Jett
January 15, 1790,	William Saunders and Agnes Jeffries
March 31, 1790,	Benjamin Shumate and Winny Gregory
———	Thomas Stribling and Elizabeth Ayers
August 7, 1790,	Zachariah Selman and Janney Lawrence
August 7, 1790,	James Kirby and Nancy Campbell
October 12, 1790,	Patrick Powers and Caty Snyder
March 24, 1790,	William Scott and Mary Ann Sullivan
February 4, 1790,	Claibrone Smoot and Mary Payne
February 23, 1790,	James Stanford and Judith Burroughs
February 20, 1790,	William Sullivan and Ann Jones
March 13, 1790,	William Robinson and Susanna Soe
February 22, 1790,	Burtis Ringo and Hannah Rector
November 22, 1790,	John Taylor and Catherine Taliaferro Buckner
October 19, 1790,	William Tolls and Diana Be———
July 8, 1790,	Reuben Triplett and Margaret French
January 23, 1790,	James Robinson and Molly Robinson
May 4, 1790,	Harris Whitecotton and Margaret Shumate
January 12, 1790,	Henry Warder and Ann Ford
November 3, 1790,	John Wright and Ann Mason
December 27, 1790,	Richard Williams and Molly Hudnall
February 15, 1790,	Henry Wey and Molly Crupper
January 28, 1790,	David Wright and Nancy Martin
——— 24, 1790,	Benjamin Grigsby and Alice Browning
January 8, 1790,	William Goff and Frances Weaver
December 7, 1790,	Robert Gibson and Sinah Newby

May 7, 1790,	James Grooms and Sarah Crump
November 22, 1790,	Robin Gaunt and Sarah Smith
September 7, 1790,	Jacob Cornwell and Molly Hayes
November 23, 1790,	John King and Ann Bethel
April 15, 1790,	Joseph Allen and Jane Bradford
October 26, 1790,	Sealy Moss and Jenny Glasscock
January 21, 1790,	Abraham McDaniel and Rebecca Boyce
March 29, 1790,	Archibald McDonald and Mary Lowry
August 24, 1790,	William H. McNeal and Elizabeth Kearns
May, 15, 1790,	Thomas Mason and Caty Singleton
April 26, 1790,	James Mackarel and Sally Morgan
January 22, 1790,	John Marshall and Rachael Boun
November 16, 1790,	William Murphy and Sally Bowen
November 6, 1790,	Michael German and Ann Masters
September 13, 1792,	Jacob Weaver and Molly Norman
October 28, 1754,	John Verell and Susan Moore, spinster

Sussex County

December 24, 1754,   Francis Hobson and Frances, daughter of Charles Judkins

October 14, 1754,   James Boisseau Jones and Ann, daughter of Hinchia Gilliam

February 10, 1755,   William Thweatts and Jane, daughter of Ephraim Parham

July 18, 1755,   John Sammon and Lucy, daughter of Robert Seat

January 13, 1755,   Nicholas Edwards and Mary Nicholson, widow

September 18, 1755,   William Parham and Mary, daughter of Edward Stevens, decd.

May 3, 1756,   Fred. Raines and Frances, daughter of James Wyche, decd., consent of her guardian William Johnson

December 17, 1756,   William Blunt and Ann, daughter of Robert Nicholson

February 16, 1756,   Peter, son of Samuel Lee, and Celia Pettway

February 14, 1756,   John Hardaway and Rebecca, daughter of Richard Pepper

February 9, 1756,   John Bonner and Mary Briggs, widow

March 15, 1756,   John Hunt and Mary, daughter of John Tyus

July 20, 1756,   William Edwards of Brunswick, and Sarah Edmunds, daughter of Thomas Edmunds. J. Edmunds consents to marriage of his sister and ward

September 24, 1757,   Col. John Nash, Sr., of Prince Edward, and Elizabeth, daughter of Charles Fisher, decd.

November 27, 1757,   Halcott Pride of Dinwiddie Co., and Mary, daughter of Capt. Howell Briggs

June 24, 1757,   Joel Freeman and Patty, daughter of William Richardson

August 19, 1757,   Henry Edmunds of Parish of St. Andrews Brunswick Co., and Sarah Briggs of Surry

July 16, 1757,   Jesse Jones and Alice Stagg

October 9, 1758,   Abram Green and Ann Blunt, widow

October 9, 1758,   Nathaniel Parham and Celia Lee, widow

29

January 9, 1758, William Howell and Hannah, daughter of George Wyche, decd.

September 27, 1758, Capt. Henry Harrison and Elizabeth, daughter of Capt. Richard Avery

July 22, 1758, John Jones and Elizabeth, daughter of Charles Binns

May 20, 1758, Benamin Wyche and Elizabeth, daughter of Samuel Peete

March 17, 1758, Lewis Brown and Martha, daughter of Wm. Richardson, decd.

March 17, 1758, John Chappell and Mary, daughter of Thomas Hines

February 25, 1758, Thomas Newsum and Alice Stagg, spinster

February 7, 1758, Joshua Ford of Southampton and Mary Caelia Thorp, daughter of Joseph Thorp.

November 24, 1759, David Tucker and Athalia Kezia Hunt, widow

July 2, 1759, Christopher Rives and Elizabeth Mason, spinster

October 25, 1759, Joseph Dennis and Lucretia, daughter of Matthew Parham

April 2, 1759, Richard Lanier and Ann Mason, widow

March 16, 1759, Henry Gee and Frances, daughter of Ephraim Parham

January 27, 1759, Charles Collier and Susanna Smith, daughter of William Smith. Letter from her brother Josiah Smith, executor of his father Wm. Smith, stating his sister Susanna was born in 1737

January 5, 1760, Robert Pettway and Phebe, daughter of Edward Pettway

February 26, 1760, James Adams and Ann Harper, widow of Wyatt Harper

February 9, 1760, Thomas Parker and Sarah, daughter of William Parker

August 18, 1760, Holman Southall and Elizabeth, daughter of William Dancy

June 9, 1760, John Mason, Jr., and Elizabeth Gee, spinster

October 15, 1761, George Wyche and Margaret———

November 13, 1761, Burrell Bowles and Mary Mason

December 1, 1762, John Cargill and Sarah, daughter of Capt. Richard Avery

December 7, 1762, Edmund Jones and Rebecca, daughter of William Johnson

October 5, 1762,   John Raines and Amy Mitchell, widow

May 24, 1762,   William Briggs and Mary, daughter of Reuben Cooke

May 20, 1762,   John Moore and Mary, daughter of Edward Smith

May 5, 1762,   Michael Nicholson and Mildred, daughter of George Cheeseman, decd.

November 19, 1764,   William Blunt and Martha, daughter of Dr. Samuel Peete

April 9, 1762,   William Ruffin and Sarah, daughter of Richard Hill

February 24, 1762,   Hartwell Phillips and Jane, daughter of John Hancock

June 9, 1762,   George Rives and Sarah, daughter of Thomas Eldridge

June 22, 1763,   Drury Burge and Elizabeth Dunn

June 17, 1763,   John Blow and Mary, daughter of George Briggs. John Thomas, guardian of John Blow, states he was 21 years July 7, 1762

May 26, 1763,   Abram Mitchell and Elizabeth, daughter of William Hines

May 19, 1763,   Thomas Peebles and Mary Hancock, widow

May 7, 1763,   John Nicholson and Elizabeth, daughter of John Andrews

February 28, 1768,   William Biggins and Molly, daughter of Sarah Biggins, widow

February 12, 1763,   Timothy Rives and Catharine Barker, widow of Henry Barker

April 21, 1764,   John Peterson of Brunswick, and Elizabeth, daughter of George Briggs of Sussex

November 15, 1764,   Ephraim Parham and Hannah Hill

December —, 1764,   John Shands and Priscilla Shands, daughter of William and Priscilla Shands

June 29, 1764,   Robert Owen and Lucy, daughter of Silvanus Stokes

October 19, 1765,   James Jones and Rebecca, widow of Edward Jones

June 20, 1765,   Thomas Butler and Mary Norris, infant

March 22, 1765,   Thomas Hunt and Dorothy Vaughan

July 4, 1765,   Jesse Hare of North Carolina and Betty, daughter of James Renn

August 15, 1765,   William Gary and Boyce Gee

October 24, 1765,   John Pettway and Fanny, daughter of Sarah
    Biggins

January 29, 1765,   John Barker and Lucy Wallace

October 25, 1765,   Thomas Sanders and Ann Harper, widow

October 18, 176—,   William Moore and Elizabeth Fluner, spinster

February 1, 1766,   Hugh Belsches and Martha, daughter of Richard
    Avery

November 9, 1766,   Benj. Blunt, orphan of Richard Blunt, and
    Frances, daughter of George Briggs

November 17, 1766,   George Kerr and Elizabeth Briggs

September 26, 1766,   Thomas Young and Katherine Barlow,
    widow

May 30, 1766,   John Avery and Ann Hill, widow

February 20, 1767,   William Johnson and Agnes Battle, spinster

November 11, 1767,   Aaron Vinson and Sarah, daughter of John
    Osburn, Jr.

August 11, 1767,   Lawrence Smith and Mary Briggs, widow

November 20, 1767,   Edward Edwards and B——Brookwell

June 2, 1767,   John Justice and Sarah, daughter of Reuben Cook

May 21, 1767   Frederick Dixon and Nancy, daughter of William
    Hines

May 22, 1767,   William Jones and Elizabeth Hunt

April 23, 1767,   Thomas Harrison and Mary Jenkins

March 19, 1767,   Ephraim Parham and Ruth Dunn, daughter of
    Thomas Dunn

November 19, 1768,   Richard, son of Richard Cocke, and Anne,
    daughter of Col. Augustine Clayborne

November 20, 1767,   Hinchea Pettway and Mary Parker

————————, 1768,   Lewis Johnson and Mary Horn

March 24, 1768,   Joseph Renn and Ann Zells, widow

March 29, 1768,   James, son of Thomas Peters, and Lucy, daughter
    of Wm. Parker

March 17, 1768,   William Parker and Mary Peters, daughter of
    Thomas Peters

March 17, 1768,   Lawrence Gibbons and Lucy, daughter of James
    Jones

September 16, 1772,   Lewis Johnson and Lucy, daughter of Isham
    Ezell

October 7, 1772,   William Parham and Mary, daughter of John
    Kelley

September 2, 1772,   Stith Parham and Lucretia Parham, widow

"An account of marriages and ordinary licenses granted in the county of Sussex, from the 25th day of September, 1771, to the 10th day of October, 1772:"

John Irby and Rebecca Briggs

William Parham and Rebecca Hunt

Allen Hines and Frances Williams

Thomas Dunn and Sarah Hobbs

Jeremiah Bonner and Sally Hall

Thomas Chappell and Elizabeth Malone

Lewis Johnson and Lucy Ezell

Henry John Burgess and Judith Driver

Robert Tucker and Mary Ann Parham

Stith Parham and Lucretia Parham

November 16, 1769, Harry S. Nicholson and Susanna, daughter of George Briggs

April 21, 1769, Thomas Eldridge and Elizabeth Pennington, widow

July 28, 1769, Marcus Pennington and Ann, daughter of Solomon Graves

June 15, 1769, Joshua Moss and Sarah, daughter of John Pennington

June 15, 1769, Drury Parker and Mildred Clanton, aged 26, daughter of Mary Clanton

April 20, 1769, James Chappell and Sally, daughter of William Hines

April 20, 1769, Silvanus Bell and Mary, daughter of Lewis Johnson

February 10, 1769, Nathl. Parham and Rebecca, daughter of William Parham

February 17, 1769, Thomas Sisson of Brunswick Co., and Martha, daughter of William Parham, decd.

February 3, 1769, John Qessenberry and Isabella, daughter of Eliza Bedingfield

November 3, 1769, Eldridge Clack and Betty, daughter of John Hunt, decd.

March 15, 1771, Hartwell Hines, son of Joshua Hines, and Elizabeth Edmundson

June 27, 1771, William Mason and Mary, daughter of William Gilliam, decd.

August 15, 1771,   Capt. John Walker and Hannah Hunt, widow

April 10, 1771, James Nicholson, Jr., and Elizabeth, daughter of Richard Woodroof

March 22, 1771,   John Tuel and Mary, daughter of Isaac Mason, decd.

December 16, 1771,   John Irby and Rebecca Briggs, daughter of John Briggs

December 27, 1771, William Parker and Susanna, daughter of Benjamin Hunt, decd.

February 11, 1771,   Henry Blow and Rebecca, daughter of John Birdsong

March 5, 1771, Francis Ward and Sarah, daughter of Robert Webb.

March 11, 1771,   Thomas Howard and Mary Bailis, daughter of Humphrey Bailis

January 30, 1773, Robert Tatum and Amy, daughter of Charles Gee

March 18, 1773, Philip Harwood and Selah Rochel, daughter of John Rochel, decd.

December 16, 1773,   William Rives and Elizabeth, daughter of Thomas Vaughan

December 27, 1773, Lemuel Cocke and Ann Irby, ward of Richard Blunt

March 18, 1773, Chappell Gee and Rebecca Lucas, daughter of Wm. Lucas, decd.

February 8, 1773,   Timothy Rives and Martin Binns

September 21, 1773,   Richard Mason and Mary Burrow, widow

September 15, 1774,   John Cargill and Ann Eldridge, widow of Wm. Eldridge

August 18, 1774, Frederick Jones and Susanna, daughter of Aug. Claiborne

July 4, 1774,   Hamilton Jones and Jacobina Willis

June 23, 1774, Capt. James Jones and Leah Wyche, relict of James Wyche

September 18, 1774, Joel Eppes and Lucy Meachum, daughter of Banks Meachum

May 30, 1774, William Edwards and Susanna Edmunds, daughter of Thos. Edmunds, decd.

May 19, 1774,   Thomas Gilliam and Sarah, daughter of Arthur Williamson

April 11, 1774, James Chambliss and Sarah, daughter of Thomas Moore, decd.

July 25, 1774, William Mason and Lucy, daughter of Major John Mason

March 17, 1775, John Mason and Elizabeth, daughter of Thomas Peters

February 18, 1775, Peter Cole Harrison and Margaret, daughter of John Hay, decd. Nathaniel Harrison writes that Peter Cole Harrison is 21 years 18th February, 1775. Margaret, daughter of John Hay, and Judith his wife, was born the 5th day of November, 1751

June 19, 1775, William Rives and Jemima, daughter of William Heath

October 31, 1775, Henry Hartwell Marable and Elizabeth, daughter of Isaac Mason, decd.

June 15, 1775, Thomas Peterson and Elizabeth, daughter of Augustine Claiborne

October 8, 1776, Stith Bolling and Charlotte, daughter of Mr. John Edmunds, decd.

September 21, 1776, John Cocke and Lucy Herbert Claiborne, daughter of Augustine Claiborne, Esq.

January 16, 1777, Thomas Mason and Lucy Jones, daughter of Capt. James Jones

October 16, 1777, James Mason and Rebecca Thweatt

September —, 1777, Richard Gregory, son of Roger Gregory of Lunenburg, and Mary Brodnax, widow of William Brodnax

October 18, 1777, Dr. Alexr. Glass Strachan and Lucy Pride, with consent of the guardian, Colin Campbell

————, 1778, Robert Parham, son of Nathaniel, and Rebecca Berriman, daughter of John Berriman

September 21, 1778, Lewis Lanier, son of Sampson and Anne, daughter of Thomas Butler

November 5, 1779, Henry Chappell and Elizabeth Rives, daughter of Elizabeth Rives

November 15, 1779, Samuel Mangum and Rebecca, daughter of Richard Cotton

April 19, 1779, William Brent and Mary Parham

April 15, 1779, John Summers and Lucretia Jones

July 24, 1779, John Massenburg and Elizabeth Eldridge, with letter of consent from her mother, Ann Cargill

June 2, 1779, William Shands and Lucy, daughter of William Oliver

June 5, 1779,   John Mitchell and Scota, daughter of William
  Stewart
December 1, 1781,   Sampson Collier and Sarah Gilliam, widow
October 30, 1780,   Thomas Heath and Selah Rives
February 4, 1780,   Timothy Rives and Rebecca Mason
October 5, 1782,   Peyton Mason and Pattey Peebles
December 21, 1781, John Meredith of Dinwiddie, and Elizabeth
  Pennington
November 11, 1783, Thomas Blunt and Elizabeth, daughter of Dr.
  Thomas Peete
December 19, 1782,   David Thweatt and Rebecca Jones, widow
March 13, 1782,   Enoch Lewis and Lucy Barker, widow
April 17, 1783,   Buckner Lanier and Rebecca Williamson, widow

Charles City County

August 7, 1660,	John Cunliffe and Jane Mountain
August 8, 1660,	Daniel Kigan and Phebe Banks
September 16, 1660,	William Rawlinson and Jane Sparrow
October 11, 1660,	Walter Horldsworthy and Naomie Davis
September 15, 1791,	Isaac Lacy and Elizabeth Walker
June 3, 1772,	Charles Christian and Rebecca Terrill
June 16, 1762,	Brazure Williams and Agatha Johnson, widow
December 16, 1799,	Jeremiah Jackson and Nancy, daughter of John Bell
February 3, 1768,	John Christian and Mary Maynard
December 27, 1793,	Henry Southall and Elizabeth Holdsworth
January 9, 1769,	Stephen Bowry and Mary Gregory, widow
September 4, 1781,	William Clarke and Ann Leonard, daughter of Wm. Leonard
May 6, 1797,	William Howlett and Lucy Roper
June 18, 1793,	William Daniel and Polly, daughter of Martin Martin
May 28, 1767,	William Brown and Martha Bassett
August 7, 1780,	William Hansil and Judith Crew
November 26, 1770,	John Lamb and Fanny, daughter of William Finch
September 13, 1768,	William Vaughan and Ann, daughter of John Dancy
July 23, 1767,	Hubbard Wyatt and Tabitha Minge, daughter of George Minge
January 15, 1784,	Seth Stubblefield and Lucy Timberlake Southall
November 27, 1763,	Archelaus Mitchell and Mary, daughter of John Gregory
January 17, 1763,	James Hopkins and Elizabeth Marston
January 12, 1787,	John Carter and Elizabeth Collins
January 5, 1783,	William Chancey and Mary Timberlake
May 2, 1764,	John Ridlehurst and Judith Miles
December 23, 1781,	William Wright and Martha Jackson

January 3, 1785,	Levi Jenkins and Mary Waldrop
February 9, 1788,	Thomas Matthis and Rebecca Moody
January 1, 1772,	Wm. Marrable and Susannah, daughter of Joseph Weaver
December 21, 1789,	Nathaniel Maynard and Elizabeth Mathews
July 7, 1773,	Henry Skipwith and Ann Wayles
March 30, 1791,	Christopher Haynes and Anne Young
January 22, 1787,	Henry Lacy and Lucy Duke Timberlake
May 27, 1791,	Crawley Maynard and Elizabeth, daughter of David Merry
May 20, 1788,	John Timberlake and Susanna, daughter of Gideon Christian
October 13, 1773,	Richard Taylor and Lucy Gregory, widow
December 28, 1795,	Edward Walker and Nancy Lored
July 24, 1764,	William Gregory and Ann Royster
January 28, 1797,	John Minson and Ann Whitlock Wills
January 12, 1769,	John Wodrop and Mary Clarke
June 19, 1787,	Samuel Trower and Alice, daughter of Gideon Christian
May 3, 1784,	James Miles and Mary Thompson
October 26, 1784,	Henry Phillips and Frances Pearman
March 31, 1788,	William Burton and Mary Baily
April 5, 1786,	John West and Rebecca Willcox
October 29, 1779,	Lewis Crutchfield and Mildred Jamison
August 3, 1774,	John Gregory and Elizabeth Maynard
April 17, 1790,	William Bullington and Frances Bradley
March 5, 1764,	William Dennis and Jane, daughter of William Parish
April 12, 1784,	Littlebury Hardyman and Elizabeth Eppes
April 15, 1781,	John Lefrane and Jane Bolling Kenny
October 21, 1828,	Charles Alvis and Emily W., daughter of Giles Buffin
July 15, 1814,	Armistead Atkins and Nancy, daughter of Polly Plumry
February 14, 1848,	Robert Maddox and Lucy, daughter of Mary Waddill
November 13, 1828,	Joseph T. Mountcastle and Mildred Snips
October 14, 1824,	William Haynes and Frances A. E. Hall
December 20, 1821,	John T. Harwood and Mildred Morecock
December 20, 1844,	William T. Martin and Susan A. B. Binns, daughter of Bolling Binns

April 18, 1826,   Braxton Harrison and Cammilla A. M. Johnson
June 2, 1824,   Robert Freeman and Ann Hunnicut
September 15, 1824,   Benjamin Hilliard and Jenny Johnson
April 9, 1806,   Theodrick Gathright and Elizabeth Jordan
May 26, 1805,   John Parkes and Agnes Holdsworth
May 5, 1812,   Wat. H. Tyler and Eliza W. W. Walker
November 8, 1810,   Joseph Jackson and Paysey Roach
February 28, 1843,   Fleming B. Major and Sarah H. Wilcox
November 15, 1827,   John T. Marston and Frances B. Parker
May 27, 1820,   Thomas J. West and Lucy Ann, daughter of Isham Randolph
February 8, 1808,   Thomas Wilkinson and Nancy Bradley
August 16, 1821,   Will Ratcliff and Jane Blanks
November 28, 1849,   Henry Woodcock and Mary A., daughter of Miles Blanks, decd.
July 16, 1842,   William A. Ammons and Christiana A. Southall
March 14, 1842,   Henry D. Vaden and Sarah M. Stubblefield
November 15, 1805,   Michael Bradley and Elizabeth Otey
June 12, 1847,   Pleasant Day and Elizabeth Jane Whitt
May 28, 1811,   Arthur Hamlett and Sarah Crutchfield
March 19, 1818,   Thomas Blanks and Julia Warburton
March 3, 1780,   William Southall and Sarah Dudley
October 21, 1847,   Beverley W. Ammons and Jane Frances Snipes
June 16, 1825,   George Chandler and Rebecca E. Armstead
January 23, 1823,   William B. Morecock and Ann C. Edloe
July 18, 1829,   William Mahaney and Eleanor Pointer
December 28, 1826,   John A. Smith and Sarah H. Clayton
August 21, 1815,   Edward Young and Jeanette Stoll
October 26, 1812,   Samuel Willis and Hetty Fotset
November —, 1812,   Richard Apperson and ————
March 24, 1815,   Philip Wallace and Elvy, daughter of James Morris
December 22, 1824,   George Loyd and Ann Eshon
January 15, 1820,   John Craddock and Susan H. Taylor
October 30, 1806,   Thomas Batts and Betsy Vaughan
April 28, 1818,   William Phillips and Susannah Beckit
September 11, 1806,   George Woodson and Delphia White
January 4, 1813,   Elijah Crew and Sally Evans
November 27, 1811,   William B. Page and Evelyn B. Nelson
February 25, 1817,   William T. Barlow and Susannah Crew

September 9, 1811,   William Taylor and Mary L., daughter of Henry Vaughan

January 21, 1807,   Mathew Wyat Shields and Mary R. Bell

York County

December 28, 1772,	A. Purdie and Peachy Davenport
January 23, 1772,	Edward Watts and Mary Abercrombie
March 17, 1772,	R. Brown and Mary Tomkins
February 6, 1772,	William Patrick and Lucy, daughter of Edmond Curtis
January 8, 1772,	Thomas Powell and Mary Hobday
December 8, 1772,	John Moreland and Fanny Stroud
November 18, 1772,	Anthony Geohegan and Martha Lavia, widow
December 21, 1772,	Lewis Loyd and Anne Moss
October 15, 1772,	Robert Howard and Elizabeth Curtis
May 28, 1772,	Thomas Powell and Elizabeth Digges
March 24, 1772,	John Brown and Anne Geddy
February 10, 1772,	Willis Walker and Sarah Hunter
May 14, 1772,	Reuben Lilburn and Elizabeth Presson
February 11, 1772,	William Moody, Jr., and Barbary Bryan
April 22, 1772,	Sanford Pallison and Eliza Bryan
October 10, 1772,	Richard Deadman and Mary Ware, widow
September 5, 1772,	Ransome Foster and Elizabeth Coman
January 21, 1772,	William Gunter and ———————
May 15, 1772,	William Simmons and Ann Blasingham
March 15, 1773,	William Cary and Sarah Dudley
March 18, 1773,	James Dudley and Lydia Hill
January 7, 1773,	John Moss and Sarah Gibbons
January 13, 1773,	William Robinson and Frances Williams
April 13, 1773,	John Richardson and Elizabeth Hayes
April 8, 1773,	Stephen Mitchell and Margaret, daughter of Alex. Maitland
Feb. 18, 1773,	Allen Jones and Lucy Moss
February 9, 1773,	James Nicholls and Elizabeth Wyatt
October 15, 1773,	Pennuel Penny and Mary Burfoot
December 2, 1773,	James Moir and Elizabeth Diddip
January 29, 1774,	Thomas Presson, Jr., and Susanna Patrick
June 7, 1774,	Nathan Yancy and Sarah Wingham

October 20, 1774,   Robt., brother of Thos. Nelson, Jr., and Mary
Grymes
February 4, 1774,   James Davis and Elizabeth Fuller
July 12, 1774,   John Baptist and Betty Whitaker
December 16, 1774,   Thomas Orsell and Catharine Blasingham
January 13, 1774,   Richard Garrett and Mary Morland
August 29, 1774,   Thomas Cowles and Elizabeth Crawley
September 23, 1775,   Starkey Robinson and Ann Mennis
January 11, 1775,   Beverley Randolph and Martha Cocke
May 23, 1775, Thos. Gibbons and Martha, daughter of Benj. Lester, decd.
October 16, 1775,   Ambrose Jackson and Mary Cobb
March 23, 1775,   Charles Graves and Molly Powell
May 25, 1775,   Thomas Skinner and Elizabeth Ryan
April 3, 1775,   William Bowen and Mary Rudder
October 6, 1775,   Isaac Winfrey and Mary Graves
December 16, 1776,   W. Hunter and Eliz. Hunter Davenport,
daughter of William Davenport
March 4, 1776,   Chas. McFadden and Jane Lyppetit
July 1, 1777,   William Mallory and Martha Sweney, widow
December 15, 1777,   John McClary and Sarah Hansford
February 8, 1777, J. J. Cuthbert of State of Georgia, and Catharine Blair, widow, of this county
November 24, 1777,   William Howard and Ann Chisman
April 22, 1777,   Thomas Badget and Sarah Miller
February 26, 1777,   Saml. Major and Ann, daughter of Saml.
Timson
May 12, 1777,   Henry Howard and Martha Sclater, widow
February 3, 1778,   Chidly Wade and Ann Kerby
February 3, 1778, Harry Charles and Frances, daughter of William
Kerby
March 31, 1778,   William Meade and Elizabeth Bowles
July 3, 1778,   Benjamin Lester and Sarah Hansford
April 25, 1778,   Mallory Todd and Anne Robinson
April 28, 1778,   William Baker and Rebecca Bowles
July 15, 1778,   Pinkethman Musgrove and Elizabeth Holloway,
widow
January 20, 1778,   Edward Boutwell and Frances Parsons
January 20, 1778,   John Williams and Alice Banks
April 16, 1778,   John Glenn and Margaret Cunningham
February 28, 1778,   Augustine Davis and Martha Davenport

March 22, 1784	Gideon Johnstown and Frances Moore, widow
December 18, 1784,	William Balsom and Mary Davenport
May 19, 1784,	Wyatt Coleman and Mary M. Shields
November 8, 1784,	William Roane and Frances Burt
May 17, 1784,	Robert Armistead of Eliz. City, and Hannah Patrick
December 8, 1784,	Thomas Hansford and Elizabeth Lilburne, widow
September 1, 1784,	John Sandwich Terry and Mary Ellis
December 13, 1784,	John Russell and Martha Howard
November 20, 1784,	James Hughes and Ann Stanhope
July 30, 1784,	Harman Plitt and Lucy Cole
October 29, 1785,	Lewis Charles and Mary Allen
March 25, 1785,	John Chapman, Jr., and Mary Ellis
December 22, 1785,	William Coleman and Elizabeth Holt
March 12, 1785,	William Long and Mary Hubbard
September 7, 1785,	William Stroud and Susanna Cooke
September 22, 1785,	William Hardrick and Ann Goodwin
December 10, 1785,	Thomas White and Sally Davis
June 20, 1785,	Thos. Hunt and Sally, daughter of Enoch Langster, decd.
January 31, 1785,	Thos. Dawson and Mary, daughter of John Garrow
August 25, 1785,	Samuel Booth and Anne Harris
December 21, 1785,	Richard Booker and Ann Major
July 18, 1785,	Kinchin Stacy and Margaret Mason
February 22, 1785,	Henry Watkins and Mary Freeman
February 18, 1785,	William Cole, Jr., and Mary Hubbard, widow
November 11, 1785,	Francis Lee, Jr., and Rachel Baptist
December 21, 1785,	Hawkins Reade and Elizabeth Pescud, widow
May 21, 1785,	Benj. Powell, Jr., and Nancy Cobb
August 1, 1785,	John Jacob Oteer and ————
December 15, 1785,	William Russell and Mary Campbell
October 11, 1785,	Boaz Booth and Frances Harrison
February 21, 1786,	John Moss and Mary Holmes, widow
January 15, 1786,	Philip Bidgood and Margaret Randall, widow
February 4, 1786,	Charles Copland and Rebecca Nicolson
February 20, 1786,	Francis Charlton and Mary Powell
April 14, 1786,	Warner Lewis and Sarah Shay
April 22, 1786,	Colin Campbell Wells and Agatha Dickenson
April 19, 1786,	Edmond Monday and Mary Hill, widow

April 10, 1786,   John Moody and Mary Dickeson
April 17, 1786,   James Stevens and Rebecca Baptist
December 18, 1786,   James Dixon, Jr., and Elizabeth Cary Mills
November 27, 1786, Robert, son of Wm. Patrick and Mary, daughter of Edmund Curtis
March 6, 1786,   Thomas Minson and Sarah Curtis
May 8, 1786,   Edward, son of John Power and Frances Bryan
June 10, 1786,   Anthony Peters and Ann Carter
June 20, 1786,   Thomas Brend and Elizabeth Ratcliffe
July 13, 1786,   Richard Mears and Anne Penny
September 18, 1786,   Thomas Holloway and Amey Morris
September 18, 1786   Claude Vial of Hanover Co., and Rose Lilly Powell
December 18, 1786,   Johnson Mallory Ross and Mary Lester
May 2, 1786,   John Taylor and Elizabeth Moore
December 26, 1786,   Edward Brooks and Lucy Jackson
December 10, 1786,   Richard Brown and Rachel Warrington
November 15, 1786,   Robert Gillett and Sarah Castley
November 15, 1786,   Alexander Kevan and Felix Scouvement
May 9, 1786,   George Williams and Elizabeth Hill
November 19, 1787,   William Jordan and Mary Wood
December 21, 1787,   James Hill, Jr., and Sally Graves
November 7, 1787,   Higginson Lee and Elizabeth, daughter of Thos. Wynne
May 21, 1787,   James Williams and Rachel Roberts
November 10, 1787,   Abraham Cuttiller and Mary Francis
December 7, 1787, John Harris of Gloster and Frances Tyrie of Yorktown, widow
July 6, 1787,   Adam Craig and Mary, daughter of Wm. Mallory of Poquoson
August 24, 1787,   William Henley and Polly Taylor
June 20, 1787,   John Daingerfield and Frances Southall
March —, 1787,   Silvanus Prince and Elizabeth Myers, widow
December 24, 1787, John Campbell and Eliz. Wright, daughter of Benj. Wright of Yorkhampton parish
March 14, 1787,   Peter Powell and Sarah Timson
March 15, 1787,   William Throckmorton and Elizabeth Phillips
March 22, 1787,   Martin Goodwin and Elizabeth Goodwin
May 1, 1787,   J. Moss and Joanna Beverley, widow
May 17, 1787,   Minitree Orrell and Anna Creadle
June 21, 1788,   Gerard Roberts and Elizabeth Baptist

January 17, 1788,   Matthew Peters and Mildred Peters
May 28, 1788,   Kemp Charles and Elizabeth H. Cosby
May 7, 1788,   John Grant and Sarah Newman
February 1, 1788,   Thomas Powell and Mary Patrick
August 20, 1788,   William Moore and Frances Baptist
November 23, 1792,   Henry Crawley and Esther Dixon
April 23, 1792,   John Lee of Warwick parish, Warwick Co., and
    Lucy, daughter of Thomas Wynne, of Yorkhampton parish
September 27, 1792,   John Stoak and Elizabeth Manning
October 22, 1792,   Nathan Fletcher and Elizabeth Drewry, widow
July 11, 1792,   Reuben Gillett and Winifred Macklin
July 11, 1792,   William Gray and Rebecca Pate
August 20, 1792,   Richard Tool and Ann Powers
August 25, 1792,   David Jameson, Jr., and Mary Mennis, daughter
    of Charles Mennis, decd., and Mary his wife
November 21, 1792,   Joseph Bartley and Mary Ross, widow
December 12, 1792,   Aaron Russell and Susanna Stroud
May 18, 1792,   Daniel Ellis of James City, and Nancy, daughter of
    Philip Burt
June 8, 1792,   John Fox and Nancy Rogers
May 25, 1792,   Thomas Dillard of King and Queen, and Elizabeth
    Burt of York, daughter of Philip Burt
May 31, 1792,   Thomas Mutter and Ann Southall
April 16, 1792,   Henry Jordan and Anna Chellys
April 1, 1792,   George Morriss and Nancy Carter
May 11, 1793,   Thomas Blasingham and Margaret King, widow
May 21, 1795,   John Wright and Mary Cox
December 5, 1795,   Pierre Gordett and Prudence Blackstone, widow

Southampton County

May 3, 1781,	William Brown and Elizabeth Taylor
May 6, 1783,	Thomas Smedley and Ann Holdsworth
March 21, 1783,	Benj. Holdsworth and Nancy Liversford
March 25, 1783,	Richard D. Brown and Jane Gray
February 26, 1783,	Duncan McGurinan and Elizabeth Kerr
February 4, 1783,	Richard Ellis and Jane Binns
December 9, 1782,	John Stiles and May Schell
December 17, 1782,	John Ellis and Lucy, widow of Robert Price
January 20, 1782,	Joseph Canell and Milly Davis
October 31, 1782,	Thomas Edmunds and Martha, daughter of Wm. Short
April 4, 1782,	William Blunt and Mary Ridley
December 26, 1782,	Miles Carey and F. B. Petersen
October 30, 1783,	Delphin Dreed and Sally Ridley
June 24, 1784,	William Mossenburg and Rebecca Ridley
December 23, 1784,	A. Jones and Fanny Calvert
April 21, 1776,	Thos. Parker of Sussex and Jane Ridley of Southampton
December 13, 1751,	Absolom Smith and Harriet Dawson
April 3, 1760,	John Blunt and Mary Ridley
June 17, 1783,	William Smith and Elizabeth Taylor
November 11, 1782,	Francis Pepper and Susan, daughter of Wm. Harris
October 6, 1783,	Jordan Judkins and Sally, daughter of Saml. Warner
October 11, 1783,	Thos. I. Anson and Mary, daughter of Andw. Markie
October 20, 1783,	William Mellory and Rebecca, widow of Wm. Este
February 26, 1783,	Aug. Hummcutt and Bramley Hart
June 24, 1783,	Robt. Hummcutt and Elizabeth, daughter of Thomas Burns
June 17, 1783,	Charles Lucas and Eliz., daughter of Geo. Davis

June 18, 1783,   Wm. Ferguson and Tilly, daughter of Thomas
 Carrell
May 20, 1783,   James Lang and Anne Nelson
July 29, 1782,   Thos. Fletcher and Jane Copland
February 28, 1782,   Thos. White and Avarilla, widow of Allen
 Smith
March 13, 1782,   Joel ———— and Rebecca Ward
March 26, 1782,   Joseph Cannon and Lucy Boarman
March 26, 1782,   Hartwell Johnson and Susan Emery
March 26, 1782,   Jeremiah Williams and Martha Mitchell
May 3, 1782,   John Causaly and Lucy, daughter of Job Avenis
December 25, 1781,   James Bell and Winnie Sheffield
January 12, 1782,   Job Lucas and Sarah Andrews
July 18, 1790,   Wm. Washington and Peggy, daughter of Edw.
 Tyler
March 10, 1774,   Reub. Washington and Jean Olliver
December 30, 1773,   Henry Farrar and Diana Suffer
April 9, 1778,   Thomas Ridley and Annie Scott
November 6, 1787,   James Washington and Celia Hancock
February 20, 1796,   Wm. Washington and Betsy Stewart
January 7, 1792,   Amos Washington and Pamela Brand
January 26, 1815,   Wm. B. Moser and Rebecca J. Moser
June 22, 1815,   Francis Ridley and Louisa Blunt
January 20, 1803,   Ethelred Wright and Sally Brand
February 24, 1803,   Richard B. Kelto and Elizabeth M. Burgess
January 17, 1803,   Ethelred Washington and Sarah Brand
October 30, 1812,   Benj. Washington and Tilly Williams
April 14, 1801,   John Washington and Polly Williams
August 28, 1818,   Miles Washington and Margaret Wilson

Lancaster County

October 5, 1721,   Charles Burges and Frances, daughter of Anne
Fox

September 4, 1722,   Ezekiel Gilbert, York Co., and Winefred,
daughter of Robert Gibson

February 2, 1717,   Thomas Yerby and Hannah Degges

November 2, 1721,   William Keene and Mrs. Elizabeth Ball

May 2, 1727,   Joseph Chinn and Mrs. Elizabeth Ball

August 24, 1719,   Simon Sallard and Blanche Kelley

October 11, 1727,   Isaac White and Mary Ann Ewell

March 14, 1723,   William Cammell and Sarah Shelley

March 16, 1717, Nicholas Hack of Northumberland Co., and Eliz.
Howson. Consent of Sarah Ball to daughter Eliz. Howson's,
marriage

October 11, 1720,   Isaac Bush and Hannah Sammon

November 10, 1722,   Leonard Howson and Ann Fleet

December 16, 1717,   Wm. Sydnor and Rachael Davenport

January 7, 1723-24,   Wm. Brent and Margaret Haynes

December 21, 1723, Samuel Raine and Hagar, daughter of John
Davis

October 14, 1723,   John Selden and Mrs. Sarah Ball

November 13, 1722,   Thos. Hunton and Mary Curile

August 23, 1723,   John Rogers and Jane Walker, widow

May 20, 1727,   Robert Biscoe and Eliz., daughter of Henry
Lawson

July 11, 1719, Richard Chichester, Esq., and Ann, widow of Wm.
Fox

September 8, 1724,   Samuel Milehan and Martha Gardner

January 13, 1717,   Thos. Carpenter and Mary Nichols

March 8, 1726,   Joseph Brosier and Mary Harris

———— 13, 1725, John Selden and Sarah, daughter of Richard Ball

December 16, 1724, Capt. Wm. Balendine and Mary Ann Ewell

May 5, 1724,   Christopher Garlington and Eliz. Conway

February 17, 1723,   Wm. Ball, Jr., and Mrs. Margaret Ball

August 4, 1722,   Thomas Edwards and Sarah Swan

April 13, 1720, George Glasscock and Judith, daughter of Wm. Ball

September 30, 1726,   Hugh Brent and Eliza Morris

November 25, 1717,   Samuel Ball and Anne Tayloe

June 12, 1727, John Steptoe, Jr., and Johanna, daughter of Joan Lawson

August 12, 1724,   Mark Bannerman and Katherine Barker

———— —, 1717,   Christopher Stevens and Eliz. Armes

March 1, 1724,   William Sydnor and Catherine Taylor

July 2, 1722,   John Brown and Eliz. James

October 16, 1727, Wm., son of Wm. Montague and Mrs. Hannah Ball, daughter of Sarah Ball

December 10, 1718,   William Miller and Martha Taylor

May 18, 1717,   Richard Harrison and Ann Reade

February 6, 1718,   Jerome Pasquet and Lycia King

July 26, 1727,   James Brent and Catherine Martin

June 26, 1722,   Capt. Robert Galbraith and Margaret Carter

June 11, 1724,   John Loyal and Mary Taylor, daughter of Ann Burke

November 8, 1721, Charles Lee of Wiccocomico, Northumberland Co., and Mrs. Eliz. Pinkard

November 16, 1724,   Bryan Phillips and Eliza Stott

August 10, 1724,   James Carter and Mary Brent

September 22, 1724, Denis McCarthy and Sarah Ball, daughter of Wm. Ball

January 14, 1723-4,   Thomas Chilton and Winifred, daughter of Judith King

June 28, 1723,   William Hobson and Judith Fleet

August 14, 1724,   Eaton Reeves and Priscilla Palmer

May 24, 1727. David Ball and Ellen, daughter of George Heale

October 17, 1723, Presley Cox and Mary, daughter of Henry Fleet

February 10, 1717,   Wm. Nash and Ann Kirk

November 1, 1718,   Wm. Fleet and Ann Jones

July 22, 1734,   Wm. Heale and Judith Swan

October 26, 1739,   Chichester Chinn and Agatha Thornton

September 21, 1737, Griffin Fauntleroy, Jr., and Mrs. Judith Heale

November 15, 1737,   Thomas Hunton and Ann Wall

July 3, 1734, Richard Chichester and Ellen, daughter of Wm. Ball

April 9, 1735,   Wm. Brent and Letitia Wale

August, 1734, Merryman Payne, son of Judith Payne, and Catherine Brent

January 3, 1736-7, Anthony, son of Wm. and Catherine Sydnor, and Eliza Taylor

September 22, 1736,	Charles Ewell and Sarah Ball
June 10, 1729,	Robert Edmonds and Anne Conway
July 13, 1736,	John Edwards and Ann Swan
June 20, 1735,	Robert West and Margaret Buckles
April 15, 1737,	James Scrosby and Eliz. Lee

January 16, 1732, Mr. George Braxton and Mary, sister of John Carter

October 5, 1734,	Le Roy Griffin and Mrs. Mary Ann Bertrand
March 12, 1736-7,	Stokely Towles and Eliz. Martin
March 19, 1730,	Francis Timberlake and Judith Lawson
December 10, 1737,	Jesse, son of James Ball, and Mrs. Frances Burges

May 7, 1735, Adam Dickie and Ann Thacker of Parish of St. Mary's White Chapel

June 4, 1737,	Joseph Wharton and Ann Edmonds
June 14, 1736,	George Ball and Anna, daughter of Eliz. Taylor
August 19, 1732,	Arthur McNeale and Eliz. Frizzel
January 9, 1733,	John Hill of Northumberland, and Eliz. Martin
August 10, 1731,	John Woodson and Mary Miller
March 12, 1735-6,	Thomas Perkins and Elinor Currell
April 22, 1730,	Thomas Scott and Susanna Odor, widow
October 13, 1729,	George Payne and Frances Edwards
March 26, 1728,	Presley Cockarell and Susannah Whaley, widow

July 26, 1718, Mann Page and Judith, daughter of Robert Carter

July 28, 1730, Henry Fitzhugh, Jr., of Stafford and Lucy, daughter of Robert Carter

February 4, 1737-8,	John Norris and Jane Cammell
September 12, 1720,	John Dameron and Eliz. Taylor

January 8, 1727-8, Jas. Pendleton of Drysdale Par., King and Queen Co., and Mary Lyell, widow

April 10, 1728, Wm. Glascock of Richmond Co., and Esther, daughter of Sarah Ball

December 10, 1735,	George Ball and Judith Payne
October 25, 1738,	Robert Newsom and Behethlan Jones
November 12, 1735,	Thos. Chinn and Sarah Mitchell
July 6, 1730,	Wm. Edwards and Eliza Grigg

January 15, 1736,   John Cannaday of Maryland and Katherine Heale

February 18, 1734,   Lindsay Opie and Sarah Heale, daughter of George Heale

January 11, 1746,   Thomas Flint and Hannah Blakeman

June 12, 1747,   Wm. Downman and Ellen Chichester, widow

December 16, 1746,   Thos. Taylor and Eve, daughter of James Ball

August 6, 1742,   Adam Crump of Prince William Co., and Hannah Heale

July 15, 1748,   John Bell and Frankey Edmonds

October 16, 1747,   William Hainey and Ann Edwards, widow

April 14, 1749,   Newton Keene and Sarah Edwards

December 13, 1745,   Gavin Lowry and Behethlan Newsom

November 21, 1746,   Richard, son of John Selden, and Mary, daughter of James Ball

January 10, 1746,   Solomon Ewell and Eve Taylor

August 3, 1744,   John Mitchell and Charity Coleman

December 20, 1736, Moore, son of Wm. Fauntleroy, and Ann Heale

January 9, 1733,   James Robb and Frances Buckles

February —, 1728-9,   Rev. Charles Smith of Wiccocomoco and Eliz. Chilton

May 29, 1746,   John Fleet and Mary Edwards

September 30, 1747,   John Jones and Sarah, daughter of Margaret Ball

August 1, 1749,   Ezekiel Gilbert and Elizabeth Lawson

September 11, 1747,   Edward Blackmore and Hannah Revills

June 30, 1746,   Nathaniel Carpenter and Frances Blakerley

April 6, 1745,   William Kelly and Elizabeth Riley, widow

July 5, 1749,   Kendall Lee and Betty Heale

July 15, 1749,   Ephraim Hubbard and Susannah Edwards

January 27, 1749,   William Montague and Jane (?) Ballendine

May 4, 1749,   Anthony Kirk and Sarah Brent

December 5, 1748,   Baldwin Mathews Smith and Frances Burges

March—, 1740,   William Jones and Ann, daughter of John Bell

November 15, 1750,   William Stamps and Ellinor Brent, Jr., daughter of Catherine Brent.

January 20, 1746,   George Heale and Sarah Smith

April 22, 1746,   Tunstall Hack and Hannah Conway

September 7, 1748,   Robert Mitchell and Miss Hannah Ball

January 10, 1746, John Wormeley of Middlesex Co., gent., and Miss Ann Tayloe, daughter of William Tayloe.

January 13, 1748, George Glascock of Richmond Co., and Judith Mitchell.

April 17, 1753, William Yerby and Frances, daughter of Robert McTyre.

July 6, 1756, Francis Christian and Katherine, daughter of Ann Chinn.

April 15, 1757,	Isaac Eustace and Agatha Conway
June 22, 1753,	John Bond and Sarah Sharpe
June 7, 1759,	Richard Chichester and Anne Gordon
June 20, 1757,	Col. John Payne and Jean Chichester
November 27, 1758,	Andrew Robertson and Ellen Chichester
May 17, 1756,	William Hubbard and Eliza Boatman
May 15, 1756,	Daniel Clark and Anne Sheldon
April 7, 1758,	John Curd and Lucy Brent
February 15, 1762,	Edney Tapscott and Mary Shapleigh
December 16, 1763,	Jonathan Pullen and Betty Anne Brumley

November 11, 1761, John Smither and Lucy, daughter of Thomas Carter.

February 19, 1762, Moses Lunsford and Ann Payne

July 26, 1762, Capt. Thomas Snail and Elizabeth Weathers Haynes, orphan of James Haynes, Jr.

June 19, 1762,	Robert Edmunds and Elizabeth Lee Taylor
June 17, 1761	John Dillard and Hannah McTyre
July 28, 1764,	Leroy Griffin of Richmond Co. and Alice Currie

December 11, 1764, Travers Downman of Wiccomico, Northumberland and Anne Conway

March 10, 1764,	John Bass and Mary Degge
January 20, 1764,	Richard Payne and Ellen Bailey
October 16, 1764	Thomas Chinn, Jr., and Sarah Brent

January —, 1764, William Steptoe and Betty, daughter of George Yerby

February 11, 1758,	Henry Tapscott and Mary Shearman
December 9, 1754,	Francis Milner and Betty Ball
January 14, 1751,	Edward Carter and Katherine Brent
October 1, 1751,	John Neale and Helen Harper
February 20, 1750,	Robert Edwards and Anne Chinn
September 1, 1750,	Edward Rogers and Katherine Edwards

July 11, 1744, Dr. Joseph McAdam and Sarah Anne Pinkard, of the parish of Wicocomico, Co. Lancaster, widow

June 29, 1756,   Rawleigh Shearman and Elizabeth Gilbert
January 20, 1759,   Thomas Glascock and Mary Ball
January 20, 1752, William Glasscock, Jr., and Elizabeth Chichester
December 20, 1756, Richard Stephens and Frances Payne, daughter
     of George Payne
July 11, 1752,   Thomas Chinn and Mrs. Anne Edwards
July 24, 1753, Josiah Carter and Betty Doggett, daughter of William
     Doggett
May 19, 1758,   Thaddeus McCarty and Ann Chinn
July 18, 1750,   Nicholas Currell and Margaret Lawson
January 15, 1750,   Thomas Carter and Ann Hunter, widow
October 20, 1753,   John Yerby and Betty Yerby
December 31, 1751,   Spencer Currell and Judith Bridgeford
August 9, 1758,   Henry Carter and Hannah Chilton
September 6, 1750,   Hugh Brent and Susannah Payne
November 9, 1750,   Edward Blakemore and Jennie Neasum
July 7, 1749, Kendall Lee and Betty Heale. Consent of mother,
     Priscella Chinn, to daughter's marriage
November 19, 1754, John Muse of Westmoreland Co., and Frances
     Chattin.
May 1, 1753,   William Brent and Judith King, widow
August 21, 1758,   George Flower and Lucy Brent
March 23, 1754,   John Smith and Anne Neasum
December 20, 1763,   Bartley James and Elizabeth Hathaway.
October 16, 1762,   William Powell and Nancy Steptoe
July 4, 1764,   William Steptoe and Betty Woodbridge Yerby
June 18, 1762,   Nicholas George and Frances Connaly
July 16, 1762,   William Payne and Lucy George
December 28, 1764,   William Chowning and Thomasine Sharpe
January 7, 1762, Martin Shearman, Jr., and Mary Hunt, with con-
     sent of Eliza Stott, mother of Mary Hunt.
March 20, 1762, Charles Rogers and Catherine Brent. Consent of
     Edward Carter to marriage of his wife's daughter, Catherine
     Brent.
October—, 1761,   Hugh Brent and Esther Shearman
July 16, 1764,   Maurice Brent and Lucy Flower
January 20, 1762,   John Leland and Lucy Lee
March 22, 1762, William Pollard and Betty Brent. Consent of Ed-
     ward Carter, guardian of Betty Brent, orphan of Hugh Brent,
     decd.
September 23, 1762,   Will Churchill and Elizabeth Edwards

August 27, 1762,   James Kirk and Mary Norris
January 9, 1762, William Schofield, son of William Schofield, and
     Judith Purcell
July 10, 1764, Thomas Beale and Jane Currie, daughter of David
     Currie
June 9, 1763,   James Creswell and Mary Garlington
December 18, 1762,   James Ewell and Mary Ewell
June 20, 1760,   James Montague and Elizabeth Chinn
May 13, 1760, James Nuttall and Sarah James, daughter of Thomas
     James.
December 1, 1766,   Ben Waddey, Jr., and Margaret Payne
May 26, 1768,   Isaac Pitman and Margaret James
June 8, 1765, Fortunatus Sydnor and Elizabeth Sharpe. Consent of
     John Ball to ward's marriage
March 9, 1765,   Jesse Ball and Agatha Conway
March 12, 1765, John Ball and Mary Ball. Consent of Lettice Ball,
     mother of Mary Ball, and of Williamson Ball, guardian to
     his brother, John Ball
April 24, 1765, Leroy Pope and Elizabeth Mitchell. Leroy Pope
     age 23 the 21st Aug. and Elizabeth Mitchell is 22 years old
November 4, 1768,   James Brent and Sarah Cammell
November 24, 1769,   William Mitchell and Mary Miller
August 18, 1769,   Mungo Harvey and Priscilla Ball
October 7, 1767, James Waddell and Mary Gordon, daughter of
     James Gordon
October 22, 1765, Samuel Downing and Mary Robertson, daughter
     of Dr. Robertson
September 3, 1765, George Phillips and Mary Yerby, with consent
     of Elizabeth Woodbridge Yerby.
March 18, 1765,   Thomas Stott and Betty Stoneham
October 21, 1768, Henry Lawson and Esther Chinn, with consent
     of Robert Chinn
November 17, 1768,   Fleet Henton and Katherine Pope
November 19, 1767,   Jesse Chilton and Ann Smith
May 6, 1768, Thomas Griggs and Judith Kirk, with consent of her
     mother, Sarah Kirk
January 7, 1768, William Lewis and Anne Sharpe, with consent of
     her mother, Sarah Bond
September 5, 1765,   Rawleigh Carter and Sarah Sharp
March 10, 1768, Joseph Shearman and Susanna Chinn, with consent
     of Robert Chinn to his sister's marriage

May 19, 1768,   Henry Towles and Judith Haynes

March 6, 1769,   James Webb and Mary Holden

January 3, 1769,   James Simmons and Elizabeth Hammond

November 16, 1769, William Nutt of Northumberland, and Mary Downing of Lancaster

December 1, 1769,   John Nichols and Mary Townsend

December 16, 1769, Francis Humphrey Christeen and Anne Shearman, with consent of M. Shearman and Ann Shearman to daughter's marriage

August 24, 1769,   Henry Chowning and Eunice Bailey

May 19, 1768,   James Kirk and Lucy Carter

December 9, 1768,   William Mott and Elizabeth Hubbard

June 17, 1765,   John Bailey and Judith Brent

December 30, 1766, John Duns, Jr., and Caty McTyre, with consent of her father, Robert McTyre

August 18, 1766,   Thomas Flint and Silla Routt

June 23, 1766,   Henry Hinton and Anna Fleet

December 18, 1770, Francis Jones of Warwick Co., and Jane Armistead of Lancaster

December 31, 1774, Thomas Hunton and Elizabeth Hinton, widow

January 21, 1773, Richard Payne and Ann Shearman, with consent of her mother, Ann Shearman

January 22, 1772, Nicholas Pope and Elizabeth Fleet, with consent of her father, John Fleet

April 16, 1772,   Daniel Muse and Jean Robinson

October 5, 1772,   William Steptoe and Joanna Doggett

November 11, 1772,   Edwin Lunsford and Mary Carter

November 21, 1771,   Thomas Carter and Elizabeth Doggett

September 16, 1773,   John Dye and Sally Dye

October 26, 1774,   Thomas Brent and Judith King, widow

October 11, 1774,   William Kenner and Betty Myers

March 5, 1771,   John Eustace Beale and Elizabeth Lee

July 17, 1771, John Payne and Bridget Blakemore, with consent of her father, Edw. Blakemore

March 4, 1771, Charles Lee's consent that Mr. John Beale may marry his daughter, Elizabeth Lee

February 26, 1774, Rodham Lunsford and Lettice Carter, widow

November 3, 1772, Le Roy Griffin and Judith Ball, daughter of James Ball

December 11, 1772, William Montague and Lucy Smith, relict of Baldwin Smith

August 13, 1777, James Gordon, Jr., and Elizabeth Gordon, spinster.
Consent of James Gordon to marriage of his sister, Elizabeth

April 15, 1775,   Charles Rogers and Peggy Chowning
May 9, 1777,   Gavin Lowry and Hannah Chowning, widow
February 16, 1775,   John Maxwell and Frances Brent, spinster
December 31, 1777,   John Richards and Mary Hunton
October 19, 1780,   Jeduthan George and Danas Tapscott
Aug. —, 1783,   Rawl Tapscott and Anne Shearman
February 23, 1784,   Martin Shearman and Alice Tapscott
March 21, 1784,   Oliver Tapscott and Winifred Lunsford
November 16, 1780,   George Carter and Elizabeth James
April 13, 1780,   William James and Nancy Ellett
May 25, 1780,   James Brent and Elizabeth Hunt
May 18, 1780,   William Chetwood and Betty Neale
February 1, 1780,   Thomas Lee and Elizabeth Currell
October 21, 1784,   John Lewis and Ann S. Lawson
August 19, 1784,   John Wormeley and Fanny Bond
June 17, 1784,   Thomas Pinkard and Anne Corbin Griffin
January 15, 1784,   George Brent and Sarah Ann Simmons
December 24, 1783,   John Wiatt and Mary Harwood Currell
September 18, 1783,   Richard Lee and Lucy Denny
August 22, 1783,   Newman Chilton and Elizabeth Edmunds
July 7, 1783,   James Ewell and Sarah Ann Conway
June 19, 1783,   Joseph Carter and Sarah Chilton
May 25, 1783,   Rawl Downman and Priscilla Chinn
March 29, 1783,   Jeduthan Pitman and Caty Webb
March 12, 1783,   William Bristow and Jemima Blakemore
January—, 1783,   George Berry and Jane Carter
December 2, 1782,   William George and Molly Morris
December 19, 1782,   Charles Lee and Mildred Henning
November 21, 1782,   John McTyre and Molly Doggett
February 21, 1782,   Thomas Mott and Winifred Doggett
December 21, 1781,   William Newby and Ann Miller
October 27, 1781,   William Nutt and Jane Swan Brent
June 16, 1781,   John Smallwood and Lucy Fleet
August 23, 1785,   John Cary and Elizabeth Williams
March 17, 1785,   John Carter and Peggy Yerby
July 22, 1785,   Epaphroditus Robinson and Milly Chilton
March 16, 1789,   Thomas Hunton and Ann Pope
February 17, 1789,   Jesse C. Ball and Peggy Mitchell
June 6, 1785,   Martin Tapscott and Mary Rouand

August 14, 1787, Richard Tapscott and Frances George, with consent of her mother, Frances George

September 8, 1786,	John Tapscott and Mary Spilman
October 19, 1786,	Richard Stott and Nanny Bush
February 16, 1786,	Edward Carter and Sally White
December 27, 1786,	James Galloway and Nancy Knight
June 24, 1786,	Vincent Brent and Margaret S. Lawson
September 19, 1786,	Oliver Stott and Elizabeth Norris
April 20, 1786,	Nathaniel Burwell and Frances Wormley
February 1, 1786,	George Johnson and Elizabeth Blakmore
December 12, 1786,	John Steptoe and Elizabeth Martin George
November 8, 1786,	John Carter and Martha Dillard
February 16, 1787,	George Lee and Frances Ball

October 31, 1787, John Gordon, Jr., and Betty Lee Ball, with consent of her grandfather, James Ball

March 23, 1786,	John Muse and Elizabeth Hayden
October 3, 1791,	St. George Tucker and Mrs. Lelia Carter, widow
April 2, 1791,	Robert Fauntleroy and Sarah Ball
March 16, 1791,	Griffin Garland and Frances Burwell, widow
April—, 1791,	John Brent and Judith Norris

September 20, 1791, John Mathews Smith and Sarah Y. Chinn, spinster

December—, 1791, Charles Brent and Catherine Kirk, with consent of her guardian, William Kirk

December 24, 1791, John Lowry and Betty Hill

July 21, 1794, William Degges of Gloucester Co., and Catherine King

December 1, 1794, Ransdell Pierce of Westmoreland and Ann Graham of Lancaster

November 30, 1794, Dr. James Ewell, Jr., and Margaret Robertson

July 7, 1794, Rodham Lunsford, Jr., and Sally Cox, daughter of Thomas Cox

May 15, 1794, John W. Hunton and Mary Pollard, daughter of James Pollard

August 13, 1788,	Presley Neale and Elizabeth Harris
October 20, 1788,	Fortunatus George and Judith Norris
September 11, 1788,	William Degges and Mary Kirk
January 7, 1788,	Anthony Sydnor and Elizabeth Chowning
September 19, 1796,	Edward Downing and Hannah Ball, spinster
August 21, 1797,	William Pollard and Nancy H. George

January 25, 1797,   Joseph Ball and Ann Currell
February 8, 1797, Rawleigh Chinn, widower, and Elizabeth Shearman, spinster

King George County

From a marriage register which is among the records of King George County:

December—, 1787,	W. T. Alexander and Lucy Taliaferro
May 30, 1791,	Charles Ashton and Peggy Colton Chapin
November 17, 1803,	Charles Ashton and Elizabeth Pratt
April 20, 1807,	George Dent Ashton and Elizabeth Bernard
December 3, 1811,	John N. Ashton and Louisa Ashton
November 12, 1816,	Nehemiah H. Mason and B. P. Alexander
December 19, 1793,	Mordecai Booth and Nancy Maddocks
May 23, 1795,	George Brent and Molly Fitzhugh
August —, 1796,	Robert Bolling and Sally Washington
November 21, 1797,	Robert Bolling and Anna Dade Stith
August 14, 1799,	William Bronaugh and Maria Fitzhugh
December 2, 1788,	Alexander Campbell and Lucy Fitzhugh
November 5, 1800,	Turner Dixon and Maria Turner
June 4, 1807,	James Edwards and Elizabeth Stuart
October 16, 1788,	Nicholas Fitzhugh and Sarah Ashton
October 5, 1789,	Francis Fitzhugh and Lucy Taliaferro, widow
October 17, 1792,	William Fauntleroy and Elizabeth Hooe
October—, 1793,	W. P. Flood and Nancy P. Washington
December 5, 1795,	Richard Foote and Jane Stuart
July 18, 1797,	George Fitzhugh and Mary Stuart
December 1, 1803,	Richard Foote and Helen G. Stuart
May 3, 1805,	George Fitzhugh and Sally Battaile Dade
July 17, 1816,	Richard Foote and Lucy Alexander
February 21, 1804,	John Garner and Atherley Taylor
March 29, 1805,	John Garner and Mary Daniel
July 22, 1809,	William Grayson and Aggy Peyton
December—, 1817,	Daniel Garner and Mary Jones
January 10, 1818,	Travis Garner and Elizabeth Jones
September 2, 1818,	Thornton A. Garner and Harriet Rose
December 19, 1819,	Stephen Garner and Louisa Rowley
May 8, 1790,	Rice W. Hooe and Susanna Fitzhugh

June 5, 1790,	Henry Dade and Jane Fitzhugh
June 25, 1790,	Robert R. Hodge and Harriet Ashton
January 2, 1804,	Abram B. Hooe and Lucy Fitzhugh Grymes
June 2, 1828,	Thomas L. Lomax and Margaret R. Stuart
April 22, 1793,	Thomas Mason and Sarah Barnes Hooe
August 14, 1793,	John Morton and Margaret Strother
June 3, 1794,	Robert Mercer and ——— Carter
June 3, 1794,	John Minor and ——— Carter
November 21, 1792,	Benjamin Parke and Jane Gregory Taliaferro
June 12, 1788,	Griffin Stith and Frances Townshend Washington
December—, 1796,	Charles Stuart and Lucy Keene Ashton
November 12, 1787,	James G. Taliaferro and Wilhemina Wishart
March 25, 1794,	John Taliaferro, Jr., and Lucy Thornton Hooe
October 8, 1795,	Presley Thornton and Susan Stith
October 2, 1800,	Francis Taliaferro and Jane Pratt
December 18, 1802,	George H. Terrett and Hannah B. Ashton
December 22, 1806,	Francis Thornton and Sarah Oldham
October 12, 1808,	John Taliaferro, Jr., and Sarah Frances Brooke
March 31, 1786,	Thornton Washington and Frances Townshend Washington
February 27, 1779,	John Washington and Mary Watts Ashton
November 3, 1800,	Byrd C. Willis and Polly Lewis
December 8, 1800,	Thomas Whiting and Harriet Washington
April 4, 1802,	Henry T. Washington and Amelia Stith
May 14, 1806,	Isaac Winston and Susan Fitzhugh Dade
February 17, 1825,	J. H. Washington and Mrs. Ashton
March 31, 1829,	Henry T. Washington and Virginia Grymes
April 25, 1803,	Henry Micou, Jr., and Eleanor Roy Mercer
February 7, 1804,	John H. Micou and Harriet Goldsmith
April 11, 1808,	Jacob W. Stuart and Peggy M. Ashton
January 5, 1815,	John Stith and Sally B. Mason
June 28, 1817,	John G. Stuart and Elizabeth S. Fitzhugh
April 8, 1820,	W. G. Stuart and Frances M. W. Stuart
February 24, 1802,	Thornton Bernard and Eleanor Ashton
April 13, 1803,	Thomas Bernard and Frances T. Stith
December 28, 1804,	William Bernard and Elizabeth Fauntleroy
July 14, 1805,	Thornton Bernard and Elizabeth Washington
May 15, 1817,	John Hooe, Jr., and Maria M. G. Beverley
December 4, 1827,	Abram B. Hooe and L. C. Fitzhugh
May 28, 1831,	William A. Harrison and Frances P. Hooe
March 16, 1837,	George M. Hooe and Elizabeth M. Stith

December 26, 1837,   Abram B. Hooe and Lucy T. Grymes
July 30, 1811,   John Conway and Mary Stuart
——— —, 1816,   Richard Foote and Lucy Alexander
May 29, 1828,   James G. Taliaferro, Jr., and E. A. S. Burd
April 4, 1831,   Thornton Taylor and Matilda Rose
February 25, 1818,   Elliott Muse and Polly T. Blackburn
April 18, 1820,   Francis Fitzhugh and Amanda F. Johnson
July 30, 1820,   Frank Thornton and Sarah Rose
May 3, 1824,   Augustine Fitzhugh and Mary M. Skinker
June 17, 1826,   Richard Foote and Ann Stuart
July 19, 1830,   J. M. Fitzhugh and Mary Stuart
August 4, 1828,   William H. Ashton and Sarah Dickenson
——— —, —,   Charles H. Ashton and Mary M. Pollard
June 16, 1846,   John B. Stith and Caroline H. Stuart
July 16, 1849,   Charles E. Stuart and R. S. Lomax
July 19, 1848,   James L. Taliaferro and Jane B. Jones
March 28, 1842,   Hugh M. Tennant and Eleanor A. S. Grymes
October 19, 1840,   John A. Hoomes and Baynton T. Fitzhugh
September 15, 1841,   W. D. Hooe and Sarah Massey
November 18, 1848,   Charles D. Lewis and Elizabeth S. Fitzhugh
May 31, 1849,   Adolphus G. Fitzhugh and Rosa P. Stuart

Surry County

January 4, 1781,	William Irby and Jane Edwards
December 26, 1780,	Jesse Cocks and Rebecca Ker
September 10, 1780,	Benjamin Ellis and Martha Eisby
September 1, 1780,	Samuel Thomas and Katherine Carrell
June 27, 1780,	Benjamin Barham and Frances Phillips
June 27, 1780,	James Dowell and Harriet Stewart
June 24, 1780,	John Owen Wallace and Elizabeth Bennett
May 20, 1780,	Job Judkins and May Rowell
April 8, 1780,	Henry Crofford and Jane White
March 16, 1780,	George Barlow and Mary Lancaster
February 23, 1780,	M. Smith and Martha Grantham
February 7, 1780,	Ward Putney and Eliz. Goodman Collins, daughter of William
December 14, 1779,	William Evans and Rebecca Dreer
November 9, 1779,	Joseph Hart and Harriet Barby
October 16, 1779,	Andrew Adamson and Sally Burn
September 8, 1779,	Isham Inman and Mary Gibbons
July 13, 1779,	Stephen Collier and Nancy Hills
April 26, 1779,	Edward Dudley and Annie Holt
January 3, 1775,	Francis ———— and Harriet Cocke
March 13, 1775,	Joel Boyton and Sarah Grantham
February 13, 1775,	Benjamin Bell and Edith Beabe
February 17, 1775,	William Mitchell and Elizabeth Hodges
February 16, 1775,	Henry Mooring and May Smith
January 24, 1775,	Richard Yarborough and Sarah Withers

Amelia County

January 24 1760,   Henry Anderson and Martha Cocke
March 4, 1768,   Robert Anderson and Jane Foster
April 28, 1768,   Polly Anderson and ——— Goode (of Prince
   Edward County)
March 28, 1776,   Elizabeth Anderson and Stephen Farmer
July 10, 1779,   Nancy Anderson and George Robertson
September 9, 1782,   Rilla Anderson and Robert Burt
August 20, 1783,   Elizabeth Anderson and Elkanah Ecols
September 20, 1783,   James Anderson and Sally Bayley
October 27, 1783,   Edith Cobb Anderson and Edward Booker
December 12, 1784,   Nancy Anderson (daughter of Elizabeth) and
   John Tabb
November 17, 1784, Worsham Anderson and Misamcot Knight
   (daughter of Charles)
December 27, 1787, Catherine Anderson (daughter of Henry) and
   Fred Jones
May 17, 1787, Susan Anderson (daughter of Charles) and John
   Walton
May 17, 1787,   Matthew Anderson and Martha Dicer
March 30, 1787,   Dorothy Anderson (daughter of Henry) and John
   Ward
August 27, 1787,   Elizabeth Anderson and Daniel Wilson
December 23, 1788,   Ann Pauline Anderson and William Powell
January 10, 1789,   Frances Anderson and Daniel Versen
May 1, 1790,   ——— Anderson and Sally Anderson Blackburn
August —, 1796,   Ann Anderson and Mead Wilson
August 3, 1778,   Mary Angell and John Baldwin
———, 1783,   John Angell and Elizabeth Hendley
———, 1789,   Elizabeth Angell and William Gauldier
December 26, 1792,   Robert J. Angell and Judith Roberts
February 8, 1760,   John Archer and Elizabeth Townes
February 22, 1776,   Henry Archer and Mary Randolph
November 25, 1767,   Elizabeth Archer and James Powell Cocke

December —, 1768,   John Archer and Anne Hall
April 11, 1767,   Martha Field Archer and Christian Cocke
May 14, 1782,   Judith Archer and William Bentley
October 22, 1782, Field Archer and Frances (daughter of Brand) Tanner
December 14, 1784,   John Archer and Ann Bott
April 2, 1790,   Polly Archer and Justance Hall
March 3, 1791, William Archer and Prudence (daughter of James) Callicott
June 19, 1794,   Richard Archer and Nancy Chastain Cocke
July —, 1799,   P. F. Archer and Judith E. Cocke
October —, 1792,   Samuel Baskerville and Statira Booker
May 1, 1776, Robert Bott and Mary Wills (daughter of Lawrence)
September —, 1761,   Mary Bentley and Edward Booker
December —, 1760,   John Bently and Judith Cobbs
April 17, 1776,   Judith Bently and Joseph Eggleston
May 14, 1775, Rachel Bently (daughter of Samuel) and Hyde Saunders
May 12, 1762,   William Bibb and Hannah Booker
October 22, 1761,   Peter Bland and Judith Booker
December 16, 1779, Clara Bland and Robert Bellamy of Prince George
March 7, 1786,   Edward Bland and Lettice Jones
April 8, 1758, Robert Bolling (of Dinwiddie) and Mary Marshall Tabb
December 24, 1782, Alexander Bolling and Mary Pryor (daughter of John)
February 16, 1786, Thomas Tabb Bolling and S. Peyton (daughter of J.)
December 5, 1756,   Purify Booker and Stephen Hardaway
——— 1761,   Judith Booker and Peter Bland
June 23, 1763,   Richard Booker and Martha Robertson
June 27, 1763,   Ann Booker and James Hill
December 4, 1764, John Booker and Susan (daughter of John) Pride
September 5, 1760,   Martha Booker (widow) and James Taylor
April 18, 1767,   Mary M. P. Booker and James Henderson
May 14, 1768, William (son of William) Booker and Edith (daughter of George) Booker
April 17, 1769,   Mary Booker and Leonard Meathan
July 27, 1777,   Jean Booker and Robert Henderson

November 13, 1778,   Elizabeth (ward of Rd.) Booker and Joseph
Scott
October 28, 1779,   Elizabeth Booker and Burton Hudson
December 20, 1780,   Sarah Booker and John Childress
January —, 1781,   Edward Booker and Mary Pride
January 28, 1781,   Frances Booker and James Hill
August 18, 1783,   E. Booker and Mary Hudson
January 3, 1782,   Grace Booker and John Walthall
October 18, 1783,   Kitty Booker and John Ormstreet
December 25, 1784,   Samuel Booker and Martha Munford (daughter of James)
December 27, 1784,   Robert Booker and Jane Hudson
February 4, 1785,   Samuel Booker and Rachel Jones
February 22, 1787,   Pinkham Davis Booker and Martha P. Pride
May 24, 1787,   Gracey Booker and Absalom Farmer
April 4, 1790,   Martha Booker and Samuel Ford
December —, 1791,   Judith Booker and Blackburn Hughes
September —, 1792,   Rachel Mannott Booker and James Turner
October —, 1793,   Mary Booker and Granville Moody
February —, 1796,   Richard Booker and Sarah Cobbs
January —, 1797,   Mary Booker and Moses Ormstreet
July —, 1798,   Judith Booker and Jesse Mosby
January —, 1798,   Hyde Booker and Moses Overton
May —, 1798,   Ann Booker and John W. Selden
September —, 1780,   Davis Booker and Sarah Booker
January —, 1799,   Daniel Booker and Mary Winston
July 16, 1764,   Edward Brand and Lucy Finney
September 20, 1764,   William Brand and Judith Scott
March 24, 1785,   Peter Brand and Judith Jones (daughter of John)
November 5, 1787,   Edward Brand and Martha (daughter of
Miles Bott)
December 20, 1788,   Obedience Brand and John Wilkinson
December 26, 1789,   Thomas Brand and Nancy Clements (daughter of John)
October 28, 1791,   William Brand and ——— (daughter of James
Callicott)
December —, 1792,   Thomas Brand and Mary Walker
September —, 1793,   William Broda and Ann Brooking
August —, 1795,   Frances Brooking (daughter of V. Brooking) and
Archer Robertson, Jr.
June 2, 1790,   W. Cameron and Elizabeth Cocke

January 28, 1769,   William Claiborne and Mary (daughter of James)
Williamson
April 4, 1786,   Ward Claiborne and Nancy Butler
December —, 1799,   Kate Claiborne and Lewis Hood
December —, 1796,   John Claiborne and Kitty Hamblen
April 14, 1767,   John C. Cobb and Rachel Smith
December 8, 1768,   Samuel Cobb and Elizabeth Munford
June 24, 1791,   Edith Cobb and Francis Asselin
February —, 1796,   Sarah Cobb and Richard Booker
December —, 1757,   Agnes Cocke and Charles Hamlin
November 28, 1759,   Martha Cocke and Theopilus Lacy of Halifax
February 4, 1762,   Elizabeth (daughter of John Cocke) and Gideon
Rucker
December 24, 1764,   Stephen Cocke and Amey Jones (daughter of
Richard)
————————   Elizabeth Cock and John Cross
February 3, 1759,   Thomas Cocke and Margaret Jones
February 6, 1781,   Anne Cock and Freeman Jordan
March 28, 1789,   Mary Cock and William Cocke Ellis
June 24, 1790,   Elizabeth Cocke and William Cannon
June —, 1794,   James Cock and Mary Lewis
September 27, 1764,   James Cooke and Ann Ford
December 24, 1784,   Thomas Cook and Martha Vaughan (daughter
of Robert)
April 16, 1785,   Sylvia Cook and Joel Motley
February 24, 1779,   Mary Eggleston and Benjamin Ward
September 13, 1774,   Ann Eggleston and Daniel Hardway
November 21, 1783,   Robert Eggleston and Judith Moulson
February 23, 1788,   Joseph Eggleston and Sally (daughter of Ever-
ard) Meade
November 29, 1790,   Elizabeth Eggleston and Samuel Farrar
November 25, 1790,   George Eggleston and Elizabeth Moran
March —, 1756,   Gerrard Ellyson and Elizabeth Ford
January —, 1785,   Martha Epes and Charles Tily
January 24, 1786,   Mary Eppes and Francis Fitzgerald
December 23, 1788,   Thomas Eppes and Kate Williams (daughter
of Thomas)
January —, 1793,   John Eppes and Martha Allen
February 28, 1760,   Elizabeth Finney and Thomas Brand Wilson
January 26, 1766,   Martha Finney and Edward Haskins
July 6, 1764,   Lucy Finney and Edward Brand

January —, 1764,   Mary Page Finney and Brand Tanner

February 28, 1776,   Ann Finney and Daniel Wilson, Jr.

March 12, 1777,   Fanny Finney and William Osborne

February 24, 1785,   John Finney and Sarah Chappel

December —, 1789,   Hannah Finney and John Walker

March —, 1797,   John Finney and Nancy Garland

May 14, 1782,   Mary Giles (daughter of William) and Samuel Jones

April 14, 1782,   Amey Giles (daughter of William) and Benjamin Moseley

April 20, 1787,   William Giles and Rebecca W. Mason

March —, 1797,   William B. Giles and Martha Payton (daughter of Joseph Tabb)

November 28, 1769,   William Gooch and Henrietta Maud (daughter of Charles Irby)

November 20, 1767,   John Gooch and Judith Radford

November 21, 1757,   Elizabeth (daughter of Leland) Greenhill and John Leigh

November 10, 1768,   Pascal Greenhill and Ann Ward (daughter of Henry)

December 12, 1763,   Lettice Greenhill and ——— Jones

September 17, 1778,   Sarah Greenhill and Peter Randolph

June 24, 1780,   William Greenhill and Elizabeth (daughter of Benjamin) Ward

February 5, 1781,   Lucy Greenhill and George Washington

December 22, 1768,   John Hamlen and Philadelphia Jones

———, 1787,   Daniel Hamlin and Elizabeth Fowlkes

Novembe- —, 1797,   Edward Haskins and Nancy Vaughan

August —, 1799,   Mary C. Hudson and Richard Royall

February 15, 17—,   ——— Howlett and Martha, daughter of James Chapell

January 29, 1757,   John Irby and Jessie Wynn

October 29, 1759,   Edward Irby (Chesterfield) and Nancy, daughter of Samuel Morgan

February 7, 1778,   John Irby and Jane, daughter of Wm. Crenshaw

January 25, 1782,   Charles Irby and Martha, sister of Freeman Epes

December 13, 1783,   Charles Irby and Nancy, daughter of Thomas Williams

November 25, 1759,   Peter Jones and Martha, daughter of Richard Jones

March 4, 1756,   W. Jones and Lettice Highmore

October 5, 1756,   Francis Jones and Rebecca Green
March 30, 1761,   Joseph Jones and Martha Bedford
September 23, 1762,   Thomas Jones and Ann Towns
September 23, 1762,   Dorothy Jones and Thomas Shore
November 9, 1763,   Wood Jones and Amy Watson
July 20, 1763,   Thomas Jones and Sarah Jones
January 9, 1765, Mary Jones (ward of Daniel) and Andrew Red-
    ford
January 30, 1769, John Jones and Elizabeth, daughter of William
    Crawley
November 18, 1769, Richard Jones (Chesterfield) and Mary, daugh-
    ter of James Robertson
November 15, 1774, Richard Jones, Jr., and Martha, daughter of
    Roland Ward, Sr.
January 26, 1786,   Ann Jones and John Hawkes
March 17, 1786,   Lettice Jones and Edward Bland
October 9, 1783,   Edward Jones and Elizabeth Jones
December 27, 1787, Fred. Jones and Catherine, daughter of Hy.
    Anderson
July 23, 1787,   Thomas Jones and Dorothy Jones
July 23, 1787,   Martha Jones and Thomas Short, Jr.
June 15, 1790,   Susan Jones and W. Wyatt
November 25, 1790,   Mary Jones and Edward Scott
February 6, 1790, Samuel Jones and Patsey, daughter of Josiah
    Eames
July 27, 1791,   P. Jones and Catherine Chappel
December —, 1792,   Ann Jones and Edward Ward
November 28, 1793,   Archer Jones and Frances Brand Scott
May —, 1795,   Prudence Jones and Edward Jones
June —, 1790,   Richard B. Jones and Frances Jones
September —, 1790,   Lewis Jones and Prudence Ward
April 12, 1775,   Peter Jones and Elizabeth Wilkinson
December 12, 1778,   Edward Jones and Martha Jones
February 12, 1777, Mary Jones (widow) and Sterling Olach Thorn-
    ton
February 11, 1777, Barth. Jones and Margaret, daughter of Row-
    land Ward
May 25, 1780,   Elizabeth Jones and Littlebury Royall
October 5, 1781,   Harrison Jones and Ann Logan
December 20, 1781, Elizabeth, sister of Daniel Jones, and Robert
    Foster

December 11, 1782, Rebecca, sister of Daniel Jones, and Stephen Beasley

May 14, 1782, Samuel Jones and Mary, daughter of William Giles

April 17, 1782, Adrian Jones and Nancy, daughter of Richard Hamson

June 5, 1783, Robert Jones and Ann, daughter of Rowland Ward

November 6, 1783, Sarah Jones and Dudley Holt

November 27, 1783, Job Jones and Sarah Turner

December 27, 1783, Abraham Jones and Lucy Atkinson Jackson

October 22, 1784, William Jones and Mary Hancom

September 4, 1784, Daniel Jones and Catherine Ward

October 28, 1784, Charles Jones and Sally Ford

November 8, 1784, Moses Jones and Frances Fields

October 28, 1784, Thomas Jones and Prudence Jones

November 24, 1785, Samuel Jones and Delphe Ferguson

July 11, 1785, Reuben Jones and Martha Marshall

April 9, 1761, Gideon Marcon and Rebecca Walker

December 9, 1768, Launcelot Mora and Hannah Walker

September 11, 1778, Francis Mallory and Frances Allen

April 1, 1765, Mary Mallory and John Tabb

February 5, 1789, Everard Meade and Mary Ward

May 20, 1781, —— Morris and Sarah Esher

December 15, 1779, William Moseley and Ann Wills

January 28, 1784, John Moseley and Ann Willson

February 28, 1788, William Moseley and Rebecca C. Townes

July 23, 1791, Agnes Osborn and Daniel Woodridge

November —, 1796, Edward Owen and Fanny Clements

November —, 1798, James Owen and Martha Claybrook

——, 1764, Susan Pride, daughter of John Pride, and James Booker

August 31, 1764, William Pride and Mary Tanner

June 28, 1781, Mary Pride and Edmund Booker

November 3, 1799, Elizabeth Welden Pride and Bennett Moxley

July —, 1799, Thomas Pride and Rebecca Pride

January 19, 1782, Elizabeth, daughter of John Pryor, and John Timberlake

September 28, 1786, Marietta Pryor and Daniel Farley

April —, 1769, Henry Robertson and Tralvena Greenwood

March 20, 1769, Frances Robertson and Lucretia Turner

June 31, 1776, John Robertson and Elizabeth, daughter of John Royall

July —, 1799,	George Robertson and Nancy Anderson
——, 1777,	William Robertson and Betty Brand Washam
April 8, 1786,	John Robertson and Betty B. Robertson
November —, 1798,	James Robertson and Mary Epes Robertson
April —, 1796,	John Robertson and Betsey Farley
March —, 1793,	William Robertson and Cynthia Ford
May —, 1764,	John Royall, Jr., and Betty Townes
July —, 1776,	Elizabeth Royall and John Robertson
December 27, 1777,	John Royall and Sarah Dennis
August —, 1795,	Richard Royall and Mary C. Hudson
September 27, 1759,	John Scott and Sara Scott
April —, 1758,	Roger Scott and Prudence Farley, of Henrico
January 14, 1783,	Sally Scott (ward of George Carrington) and Hy. Tatum
January 10, 1783,	John Scott (son of John Scott and ward of George Carrington) and Nancy Worsham
September 21, 1788,	John L. Scott and Martha Worsham
January 19, 1760,	Abram Skelton and Cloe Robertson
March —, 1762,	—— Skelton and Elizabeth Sheppard
December 27, 1776,	Vincent Skelton and Susie, daughter of Henry Robertson
October 28, 1785,	—— Skelton, Jr., and Susie Irby
January 27, 1764,	Robert Steger and Mary Dawson
May —, 1797,	Thomas Steger and Elizabeth Goose
July 2, 1760,	William Stokes and Lucretia Ellis
October 14, 1786,	William Stokes and Nancy, daughter of William Greenhow
August —, 1799,	Allen Stokes and Elizabeth, daughter of Abram Green
December 12, 1763,	Edward Tabb and Jean Clements
April 1, 1763,	John Tabb and Mary Mollony
March 6, 1784,	Reuben Thornton and Prudence Mumford
January 11, 1768,	Prudence Ward and William Mumford
April —, 1777,	Sarah Ward and Rowland Ward
April 4, 1786,	Claiborne Ward and Nancy Butler
March —, 1800,	Campbell Anderson and Polly Gordon
December —, 1802,	Dorothy Anderson and Brant Jones
July —, 1801,	Claiborne Anderson and Polly Brant Jones
March —, 1814,	Harriet Anderson and Thomas Pride
March —, 1814,	Sally (daughter of Francis) Anderson and James Wood

July —, 1819,　　Joseph B. Anderson and Sarah Scott Meriwether
May —, 1815,　　　　　Elizabeth Anderson and John Royall
August —, 1808,　John Angell and Polly (daughter of Jacob) Roberts
February —, 1801,　John R. Archer and Frances (daughter of Francis C.) Tabb
August —, 1810,　　　　　Miles Archer and Nancy W. Archer
November 21, 1821,　Frances Peyton Archer and William Eggleston
December 21, 1807,　T. Baugh and Stegora (daughter of John) Tabb
December —, 1801,　　Tinsley Bamster and Molly Shore
September —, 1814,　　John Bland and Mary B. Parkinson
January —, 1813,　Martha M. Bland and Thomas J. Parkinson
December —, 1812,　　James Bland and Mary Robertson
July —, 1815,　　Robert Bland and Caroline Pinkerton
November —, 1828,　　Edward Bland and S. Hilliman
January —, 1808,　Frances Bolling and Robert E. Meade
October —, 1819,　Harriet C. Bolling and Charles Eggleston
October —, 1814,　　Mary T. Bolling and Thomas Tabb
January —, 1800,　Judith Booker and Edward Eggleston
April —, 1800,　　Ann Booker and John E. Jefferson
May —, 1800,　Parlan Booker and Elizabeth Overton
November —, 1801,　　Mary Booker and Mathew Moseley
February —, 1801,　　Sally M. Booker and Austin Seay
June —, 1803,　Elizabeth Booker and John Robertson
November —, 1803,　　Caroline Booker and Joseph Scott
July —, 1805,　Nancy M. Booker and Archer Robertson
November —, 1807,　　Sarah M. Booker and Joseph Woodson
February —, 1808,　Rebecca Booker and Armistead T. Turner
January —, 1809,　　Elizabeth Booker and John Chaffin
November —, 1812,　Jane Davis Booker and William Brand
December —, 1812,　　Nancy H. Booker and W. H. Crittenden
December —, 1812,　W. M. Booker and Sally T. Blankensopp
March —, 1824,　　P. Davis Booker and James Dobbs
January —, 1814,　　Sally B. Booker and Peter Riscoe
December —, 1815,　　Ann Booker and Richardson Booker
February—, 1816,　Theodora Booker and Thomas Montague
October —, 1816,　　J. T. Booker and Lucy Wingoe
January —, 1818,　　Frances Booker and W. J. Scott
December —, 1821,　William M. Booker and Cene P. Hutchinson
December —, 1823,　Richard D. Booker and Nancy Jane Ford
October —, 1825,　　Caroline M. Booker and Henry E. Graves

March —, 1826,	W. M. Booker and Mary Crittenden
September —, 1826,	Isham C. Booker and Elizabeth E. Jete
December —, 1828,	Martha H. (daughter of J. T.) Booker and W. A. Willson
May —, 1817,	Lucy T. Bott and W. H. Booth
August 10, 1813,	Elizabeth T. Bott and Edward H. Jones
January 1, 1801,	Sarah Bott and Benjamin Brand
October —, 1809,	Susie J. Brand and Spotswood James
September —, 1811,	Ridley Brand and William Wills
August —, 1820,	Lucretia Brand and William Worsham
June —, 1811,	Everard Brand and Caroline James
August —, 1825,	Thomas Brand and Sarah P. Read
December —, 1801,	Edward Broda and Frances Brooking
January —, 1802,	Sarah Brooking and James Claiborne
June —, 1805,	Elizabeth B. Brooking and John Mann
February —, 1805,	Lucy Claiborne and James Wright
November —, 1800,	Nancy Claiborne and Benjamin Carpenter
January —, 1802,	James Claiborne and Sarah Brooking
November —, 1803,	John Claiborne and Elizabeth Cousins
January —, 1812,	Thomas Cobb and Nancy J. Hunt
December —, 1800,	Martha Cocke and William F. Eggleston
December —, 1817,	Elizabeth A. Cock and William Booth
March —, 1824,	Jane G. Cock and James Hobson

January —, 1825, Chastain Cock and Sarah Mead Eggleston (daughter of Everard)

October —, 1816, James H. Conway and Ann Augusta Giles

November —, 1813, John Edmunds and Elizabeth (daughter of William) Randolph

December —, 1800,	John Eggleston and Judith C. Eggleston
December —, 1804,	Ann Eggleston and William Hichman
April —, 1806,	Robert Eggleston and Ann Hill
December —, 1806,	Polly Segar Eggleston and John L. Turner
May —, 1812,	Richard Eggleston and Martha Baugh

May —, 1818, Richard B. Eggleston and Mary (daughter of Elizabeth) Tanar

April —, 1819, Alfred O. Eggleston and Anna Maud Eggleston

June 5, 1827, Judith Elizabeth (daughter of Edward) Eggleston and George Jefferson

June —, 1804,	Amy Epes and Charles Clay
December —, 1800,	Hannah Finney and Joseph Royall
June —, 1811,	Nancy Finney and Abel Moore

May —, 1820,   Anne Finney and George Markham
April —, 1824,   William Finney and Martha Wastan
March —, 1825,   May Jones Finney and John Watkins
January —, 1818,   Fanny F. Garland and George Markham
April —, 1800,   Patty Giles and Joshua Chaffin
November —, 1800, Elizabeth M. (daughter of George W.) Giles
and A. F. Townes
September —, 1813,   Rebecca W. Giles and James T. Leigh
November —, 1801,   Daniel Jefferson and Polly Bruil
April —, 1800,   Fred. Jones and Frances A. Vaughan
August —, 1800,   Wood Jones and Martha Jones
September —, 1800,   —— Jones and Dorothy Featherston
November —, 1800,   David C. Jones and Rebecca W. Jones
October —, 1804,   Sarah Jones and W. Ward
November —, 1815,   Elizabeth Royall Jones and Thomas Goode
February 26, 1816,   Seth W. Jones and Maria Hardaway
July —, 1820,   Maria W. Jones and Thomas ——
July —, 1822,   Lewellyn Jones and Elizabeth F. Webster
January —, 1824,   Fred Jones and Kezza W. Murray
July 10, 1819, Benjamin L. Meade and Jane E. (sister of Daniel)
Hardaway
November —, 1801,   Mat. Moseley and Mary Booker
April —, 1808,   Nicholas Moseley and Martha G. Ellis
January —, 1809,   Blackman Moseley and Judith Barlow
September —, 1806,   Edward Moseley and Obedience Atkinson
February 12, 1812,   W. W. Osborne and Pamella Hendrick
December —, 1807,   William Owen and Nancy Hutchinson
August —, 1801,   John Pride, Jr., and Elizabeth G. Washam
March —, 1814,   Thomas Pride and Harriet Arden
October —, 1821,   Samuel Pryor and Mary Ann Hamlin
November —, 1800, B. Randolph and Mary (daughter of Francis).
Tabb
March —, 1806,   Peyton Randolph and Marian Ward
March —, 1817, Mary (daughter of William) Randolph and
Thomas Major
April —, 1822,   Elizabeth L. Randolph and William Watkins
July —, 1825, Maria Ann (daughter of William) Randolph and
Samuel Morgan
April —, 1809,   Archer Robertson and Sarah Marshall
April —, 1809,   John Robertson and Mary E. Robertson

November 11, 1818,   William H. Robertson and Martha M. Hilcombe

May —, 1825,   John Royall and Elizabeth Anderson

January —, 1805,   William Royall and Judith Archer Royall

Middlesex County

January 21, 1742,   Beverley Randolph and Agatha Wormeley
January 9, 1749,   Henry Washington and Anne Thacker
December 29, 1741,   Mann Page and Alice, daughter of Hon. John
Grymes, Esq.
May 7, 1753,   Charles Lee and Joanna, daughter of William Morgan
May 21, 1747,   John Tayloe, Jr., of Richmond Co., and Rebecca,
eldest daughter of George Plator, of St. Mary's Co., Md.
May 6, 1752,   Christopher Robinson and Sarah Wormeley
November 20, 1747,   John Falkner and Judith Fearn
November 23, 1749,   John Armistead and Mary, daughter Armistead Churchill
October 19, 1750,   David Asselin of Gloster and Elizabeth Stubblefield
January 25, 1748,   William Meacham and Jane Aldin, widow
November 21, 1750,   Benjamin Rhodes and Dorothy Fearn
November 10, 1748,   James Gordon of Lancaster and Mary Harrison
December 15, 1756,   John Gordon and Lucy Churchill, consent of A. Churchill
December 30, 1748,   W. Owen and Elizabeth Meacham
February 15, 1748,   John Batchelder and Elizabeth Mickleborough
July 16, 1755,   Carter Braxton and Judith Robinson
May 2, 1747,   Samuel Batchelder and Elizabeth, daughter of
Thomas Laughlin
September 3, 1751,   William Stiff and Sarah, daughter James Meacham, decd.
May 7, 1751,   Rowland Sutton and Mary Ann Morgan
July 9, 1751,   Reuben Skelton and Elizabeth, daughter Lunsford
Lomax
January 1, 1749,   John Symmer and Hannah Potter, widow
September 18, 1742,   Robert Elliott and Elizabeth, daughter Capt.
Matt. Kemp, decd.; consent of Mary Kemp to her daughter's
marriage
September 9, 1741,   Bartholomew Yates and Elizabeth Stanard

75

November 24, 1741,   Cary Smith and Ann Wortham
February 4, 1742,   William Owen and Mary, daughter John Fearn
May 3, 1743, Thomas Foster and Elizabeth, daughter Thomas
    Smith, decd.; consent of Ann Smith to her daughter's mar-
    riage.
February 23, 1744, Churchill Jones and Milisent Blackburne; Eliz-
    abeth Blackburne's consent to daughter's marriage
December 31, 1743,   George Blakey and Catherine Skelton
November 7, 1745,   John Rhodes and Ann Fearn, widow
December 4, 1751,   Thomas Ivy and Anne Dudley
March 7, 1752, John Hardee and Michal Sutton, daughter of Chris-
    topher and Hope Sutton, who was born January 15, 1728
July 23, 1752,   John Yarrington and Mary Bryant
October 4, 1752,   Leonard Hill and Sarah Thacker
October 14, 1752,   Alexander Murray and Mary Clark
September 30, 1752,   James Brown and Judith Yarrington
December 22, 1752,   George Daniel and Mary Daniel
April 24, 1753,   John Blake and Elizabeth Baker
January 23, 1753,   Richard Townes and Elizabeth Burk
September 4, 1753,   George Fearn and Catherine Segar
June 26, 1753,   Thomas Saunders, Jr., and Avarilla Stiff
June 23, 1753, William, son of Robert Eastham, and Frances Bird
May 14, 1753,   Maurice Smith and Catherine Jones
April 28, 1746, Geo. Blakey of Spots Co., and Clara Daniel, widow
January 5, 1746,   Jacob Stiff and Catherine Batchelder
September 1, 1747,   George Fearn and Mary Hazlewood
October 24, 1747,   John Murray and Jane Seglar
January 8, 1750,   John Murray and Rachael Daniel
January 9, 1744,   Robert Daniel and Lucy Daniel
October 3, 1745, Charles Blocknell and Mary, daughter George
    Hardee
November 25, 1745,   Charles Hardee and Mary Carter, widow
July 25, 1745,   W. Moulson and Mary, daughter Olive Segar
February 26, 1744, James Meacham and Cassandra Warwick, widow
December 17, 1744, Stephen Tenor and Ann, daughter of John
    Rhodes
March 4, 1744, John Batchelder and Ruth, daughter of John South
June 3, 1742,   Robert Thurston and Gustant Daniell
September 7, 1743,   Jacob Stiff and Mary Meacham, widow
July 19, 1740,   Francis Beven and Catherine Cawick
August 9, 1750,   Peter Robinson and Sarah Lister

June 2, 1761, John Taylor and Elizabeth Blakey, widow
April 17, 1760, Alexander Gill and Hannah Rice
July 1, 1760, Robert Allcock and Mary Alliott
January 5, 1747, Thomas Hardin and Lucy Billups
December 4, 1758, Joseph Stephens and Anne Wortham, widow
October 4, 1758, Needles Hill and Letitia Morgan
November 10, 1758, Thomas Latham of Caroline Co. and Caroline Smith
July 3, 1740, James Bray and Frances Thacker
August 27, 1743, Charles Jones and Hannah Blackburn
January 21, 1745, Lewis Burwell of James City and Frances Bray, widow
December 31, 1744, John Fearn and Mrs. Leanna Lee
March 26, 1760, John Rootes and Sarah Reade
December 29, 1759, Richard Span and Priscilla, daughter Armistead Churchill
July 1, 1766, John Clare and Lucy Dudley
December 3, 1757, Thomas Iveson of Gloucester and Jane Montague
August 7, 1758, George Thomas of Hanover, and Dorothy Elliott
October 31, 1750, Joseph Smith and Mrs. Mary Small
June 22, 1759, George Barbee and Martha Fagan, widow
August 22, 1757, Vincent Vass of Essex, and Jane Montague, widow
December 7, 1756, Philip Rootes and Frances Wilcox
March 1, 1757, Andrew Davis, Jr., of Gloucester and Lucy Staige
May 24, 1756, Churchill Jones and Ann Kemp
May 8, 1756, Jeremiah Shepherd and Esther Daniel
November 29, 1755, Walter Keeble and Elizabeth Stapleton
October 7, 1755, John Jackson and Sarah, daughter John Blake
June 23, 1758, Thomas Kemp and Mary Smith
December 21, 1754, Robert Murray and Mary Skelton
December 24, 1754, William Mountague and Catherine Mountague
September 14, 1754, William Daniel and Susannah George
February 22, 1754, William Jones and Ann Wortham, widow
February 15, 1754, William Roame of Gloucester, and Sarah Daniel
December 11, 1753, Joseph Eggleston and Judith Segar
December 5, 1759, John Blake and Lucy, daughter of John Blake
July 13, 1760, Braxton Bird of King and Queen, and Mary Price
March 3, 1760, Henry Washington and Charlotte Montague, widow
July 14, 1760, Dudley Digges and Elizabeth Wormeley

March 5, 1760,   Stanton Dudley and Mary Berry
February 5, 1760, Richard Patterson and Elizabeth, daughter of
    William Kidd
November 3, 1760,   Henry Shepherd and Mary Daniel, widow
April 17, 1760,   Alexander Gill and Hannah Rice
July 1, 1760,   John Clare and Lucy Dudley
August 17, 1761, Thomas Fitzhugh and Mary Ann, daughter William Gardner
July 16, 1761, George West and Mary Sarah, widow of William Robinson
July 29, 1761, John Morgan and Mary Katherine, daughter William Mountague
November 23, 1761, Robert Blackley and Frances, widow Hy. Batchelder
November 3, 1761,   Richard Lokman and Mary Betty Bryant
October 7, 1761, Lewis Dudley and Frances, daughter John Aldin, decd.
September 17, 1761, Richard Davis and Lucy, daughter Wm. Hackney
November 2, 1762,   Philemon Bird and Mary Lee
December 7, 1762, John Aldin and Elizabeth, daughter George Lee, decd.
February 12, 1762, Richard Iveson and Rebecca, widow Wm. Dudley
December 7, 1762, Josiah Bream and Sarah, widow James Richardson
August 12, 1762, Thomas Fearn and Martha, daughter William Jones
September 29, 1762,   Jacob Valentine and Josia Laughlin
October 6, 1762,   John Taylor and Ann Rogers
February 23, 1763,   Marlow Dudley and Maria Ashton
September 19, 1763, George Daniel and Frances, daughter William Daniel, decd.
May 3, 1763,   Philip Mountague and Frances Mountague
August 3, 1763, Rodham Kenner and Elizabeth, daughter George Plator, Esq.
September 8, 1763,   Thomas Speir and Mary, daughter John Meacham
February 8, 1763, Thomas Reade Rootes of King and Queen, and Martha Jaquelin, daughter of John Smith, Esq.
July 14, 1763, Samuel Wortham and Ann, daughter George Wortham, decd.

December 17, 1763,   John Segar and Priscilla Hackney
January —, 1763,   Thomas Saunders and Mary Blackburn, widow
March 31, 1763,   Matthew Whiting, Jr., and Elizabeth Robinson
October 2, 1763,   Richard Daniel and Margaret Gutery
April 25, 1764, James Brown of James City Co., and Catherine
    Cheney
October 26, 1765,   Robert Thurston and Margaret Jones
January 1, 1765,   Samuel Bristow and Anne Guthery
February 20, 1765,   John Chinn and Sarah Yates
October 6, 1765, Charles Neilson and Charlotte Washington, widow
February 9, 1765,   Williamson Ball and Priscilla Span, widow
October 1, 1765,   Lodowick Tuggle, gent., and Dorothy Lee
October 22, 1765.   John Morgan and Lucy Hardin, widow
July —, 1765,   Andrew Low and Mary Roane
April 8, 1765,   Daniel Stringer and Ursula Laughton
September 3, 1765,   John George and Elizabeth Alden, widow
February 22, 1766, Captain Arthur Sinclair and Susannah Phillips
———, 1767,   Thomas Fearn and Sarah Hackney
October 15, 1772,   Churchill Blakey and Anne Chowning
November 28, 1772, Nathaniel Burwell, James City Co., and Susan-
    nah Grymes.
May 29, 1773,   Philip Ludwell Grymes and Judith Wormeley
October 8, 1773,   Benjamin Grymes and Sarah Robinson
November 17, 1773, John Blake and Alice, daughter William Hack-
    ney
December 24, 1773,   Edmund Cowles and Ann Wortham
December 15, 1774,   James Stiff and Betty Blake
October 3, 1774, Doctor George Lorimer and Hannah Thacker Tim-
    berlake, niece of Mrs. Mary Elizabeth Thacker
December 31, 1777,   James Maury Fontaine and Betty Carter
    Churchill
October 1, 1777,   Benjamin Robinson and Hannah Churchill
February 9, 1778,   William Robinson and Ann Dunlevy
May 19, 1779, Harry Beverley Yates and Lucy, daughter Rachel
    Murray
December 27, 1779, Roger Blackburn and Jane, daughter Elizabeth
    Hackney
January 4, 1782, George Lee Turberville and Betty Tayloe Corbin,
    with consent of her grandfather, Richard Corbin
December 17, 1782,   Francis Thornton and Elizabeth Hackney
December 17, 1782,   Mordecai Cooke and Elizabeth Scrosby

May 15, 1782,   William Steptoe and Elizabeth Robinson
December 16, 1782,   Richard Spratt and Anne Yates, widow
January 22, 1783,   Joseph Wyatt and Elizabeth Turner
September 22, 1783,   Thomas Griffin Peachy and Elizabeth Mills
August 22, 1784,   William Robinson and Ursula Robinson
February 5, 1784. Peter Kemp and Hannah, daughter Mary Kemp
———, 1785,   John Buckner and Dorothy Scrosby
September 14, 1788,   Philip Southall and Jane Nelson
August 2, 1792,   Richard Lee and Elizabeth Vass
December 28, 1790,   Hudson Muse and Agnes Neilson
April 30, 1793,   John Darby and Lucy Harrison Churchill
May 22, 1793,   Tunstall Banks and Polly Murray Curtis
January 24, 1795,   Carter Beverley and Jane Wormeley
January 10, 1797,   Paulin Anderson Blackburn and Sally Hodges
February 25, 1799,   William Robinson and Mary Frances Healey

Elizabeth City County

January 5, 1694-5, William Cofield of Nansimun, and Elizabeth
    Sheppard
January 12, 1694-5,   Moses Baker and Elizabeth Browne
January 8, 1694-5,   Thomas Carey of Warwick county, and Elizabeth
    Hinds
March 4, 1694-5,   William Long and Jane Proby
April 8, 1695,   Pascho Dunn and Hannah Powers
July 11, 1695,   James Wallace, clerk, and Mrs. Anne Wythe
September 7, 1695,   Thomas Harwood and Mrs. Ann Wythe, Sr.
October 15, 1695,   John West of New Kent, and Judah Armistead
October 21, 1695,   John King and Winifred Conner
——1695,   Thomas Walker of Yorke county, and Elizabeth Johnson
June 16, 1696, John George of Nansemun county, and Frances Ser-
    vant
October 2, 1696,   Thomas Harvie and ye widow Hendrick
October 27, 1696,   Charles Goringe and Elynor Allainby
November 6, 1696,   Charles Ceeley and Elizabeth Saunders
August 4, 1697,   William Minson and Paster Perrin
October 21, 1697,   William Smelt and Elizabeth Traverse, widow
October 4, 1697,   James Skiner and Jane Smith
April 5, 1698,   William Davis and Rebeccah Skiner
September 16, 1698,   William Wilson and Jane Davis
July 5, 1698,   —————— and Sarah——————
October 15, 1698,   Francis Rogers and Apphya Miller
October 8, 1698,   Martin Bean and Ann Allin
December 10, 1698,   William Sheldon and Hannah Armistead
December 10, 1698,   Richard Hurtly and Mary Naylor, widow
December 19, 1698,   John Ffrances and Mary Savoy
January 5, 1698-9,   John Cowell and Elizabeth Tucker
June 5, 1699,   John Ffryby and Mary Tucker
October 10, 1699,   John Poole and Elizabeth Sheppard, widow
——, 1699,   Thomas Gray and Bathya Crooke
October 15, 1699,   Philip Johnson and Jane Trawell, widow

December 25, 1699,	Francis Ballard and Mary Servant.
April 18, 1700,	Francis Baleman and Sarah Wood
June 14, 1700,	Nicholas Curle and Elizabeth Gutherick
June 29, 1700,	Samuel Neale and Elizabeth Exeter
February 10, 1701,	Robert Taylor and Elizabeth Hudson
March 9, 1701,	Henry Turner and Sydwell Minson
October 5, 1701,	Edward Myhill and Ann Johnson
January 31, 1701,	George Luke and Elizabeth Baskins
March 2, 1702,	Joshua Curle and Sarah Curle
——, 1702,	William Bossell and Elynor Brough
April 13, 1702,	James Pruitt and Mary Ross
——, 1702,	Colonel Miles Cary and Mary Roscow
May 3, 1702,	Bryan Penny and Bathya Gray
July 20, 1702,	Charles Jennings, Jr., and Elizabeth Westwood

YEARS 1719-20.

Leonard Whiting and Easter Minson

Thomas Wythe and Margaret Walker

Thomas Milner and Mary Selden

William Greenwood and Mrs. Harrington

George Yeo and Ellinor Boswell

John King and Rebecca Armistead

John Grieves and Ellinor Wandless

John Young and Elizabeth Ryland

Francis Mallory and Ann Myhill

Rockbridge and Augusta Counties

Performed by the Rev. John Brown, from 1785 to 1793.

November 9, 1785,   Jacob Morrell and Elizabeth Brooback
November 10, 1785,   Lewis Jordan and Mary Trible
December 6, 1785,   Isaac Trencher and Margaret McColmick
December 6, 1785,   Arthur Connelly and Jane Dale
December 14, 1785,   J. Moore and Jennie Steel
December 19, 1785,   James Risk and Elizabeth Risk
December 29, 1785,   Thomas Weles and Carrie White
January 3, 1786,   Robert Grier and Margaret Campbell
January 9, 1786,   William Carpenter and Mary Strickler
January 12, 1786,   Michael Kenady and Ellen McCaferty
January 28, 1786,   Thomas Broom and Sara Galen
February 9, 1786,   John Spence and Isabel McCormick
March 13, 1786,   Epr. Doly and July Ann Doherty
March 23, 1786,   James Paxton and Phebe McClung
April 20, 1786,   James Grigsby and Reb. Wallace
April 13, 1786,   Samuel Talford and Elizabeth Call
April 13, 1786,   Ed. Crydan and Janet Ramsay
May 4, 1786,   James Parks and Jean Buchanan
May 25, 1786,   John McCampbell and Martha Bennet

The above marriages were certified and sent to Andrew Reed, clerk of Rockbridge, June 27, 1786, by Captain Andrew Moore.

August 14, 1788,   John Collins and Mary Resner
September 30, 1788,   Ralph Wandless and Crispy Nicholas
January 22, 1789,   James Talford and Jean McCorkery

The above sent by James Brown, son of widow Brown, June 23, 1789.

September 1, 1789,   James Kelso and Betsy Sittington
October 6, 1789,   Robert Cooper and Martha Steel
November 27, 1789,   Peter Burns and Jane Miller
January 11, 1790,   Cawson McCullock and Lidia Vernon
March 16, 1790,   William Higginbottom and Polly Shannon
June 10, 1790,   William Dowthat and Anna Lewis

The above returned by myself (Rev. J. Brown), June 11, 1790.

July 31, 1790,	John Doughady and Agnes Davidson
August 9, 1790,	Luke Collins and Sarah Miller
October 14, 1790,	Alexander Thompson and Sallie Bell
December 8, 1790,	Enoch Bogas and Elizabeth McCroskry
February 22, 1791,	Joseph Walker and Grizzel McCroskry
April 5, 1791,	William Davis and Anis Caldwell
April 5, 1791,	John Bell and Rachel Foster
April 7, 1791,	Michael Miller and Christain Cline
April 28, 1791,	Thomas Paxton and Martha Steel
May 19, 1791,	David Wilson and Sarah Steel
June 23, 1791,	Joseph Shanklin and Phaney Garlon

Above sent by Samuel Brown to be recorded by the clerk of Augusta.

December 29, 1791,	Robert Martin and Mary Miller
January 12, 1792,	Arch. Musry and Sarah Fulton
February 15, 1792,	James Calhoon and Mary Lessly
May 29, 1792,	Jacob Calk and Mary McFadden

The above sent by Preston Brown.

January 21, 1793,	Richard Hay and Rachel Risk
February 17, 1793,	Daniel Moore and Martha Barnett
June 15, 1793,	William Beard and Margaret McNutt
June 22, 1793,	John Weir and Jean Spreil
September 17, 1793,	James Poague and Sarah Henry
November 23, 1793,	Samuel McClintock and Susanna King
November 29, 1793,	William Alexander and Sarah Henry

Augusta County

Note. The name of the man only is given.

December, 1749,	Charles Whiteaker
February, 1749-50,	John McGill, John Jones, George Wilson
March, 1749-50,	James Edmondson, John Ramsey, James Huston
March 19, 1749-50,	Robert Friela, William McNabb
April, 1750,	James Young
May, 1750,	Joshua Mathews
June 2, 1750,	Joseph White, Joseph Maze
April 4, 1751,	Thomas Fulton
April 15, 1751,	Edward Beard, Henry Fuler
June 3, 1751,	John Poage
June 15, 1751,	Jacob Harmon
July 11, 1751,	William Smith
September 4, 1751,	Andrew Leeper
September 10, 1751,	Thomas Milsap
August 17, 1753,	Humphrey Madison
November 22, 1753,	John Montgomerie
February 4, 1754,	John Bowyer
March 23, 1754,	Fred. Smith, John Patton
May 1, 1754,	James Bratton
July 23, 1754	George Poage, John Wilson
August, 1756,	Patrick Miller
March, 1758,	Robert Reed
July 6, 1758,	Robert Breckinridge
July 20, 1758,	Robert McMahon
August 8, 1758,	John Campbell
August 19, 1758,	Henry Murray
December 26, 1758,	John Dean
February 19, 1759,	Rob. Thompson
February 26, 1759,	John Gray
May 16, 1759,	Ed. McMullen
June 22, 1759,	James Patterson
July 3, 1759,	Samuel Love

July 14, 1759,	William Smith, James Littlepage
July 30, 1759,	Jasper Moore
August 25, 1759,	James Bell
September, 1759,	Sampson Mathews
September 11, 1759,	James Alexander
October 2, 1759,	William Fulton
November, 1759,	Michael Hogshead, David Lewis, Sampson Sayers
December, 1759,	Richard Shankland
January, 1760,	Edward McGarry
February, 1760,	James McGaffock
March, 1760,	William Davis
April, 1760,	Robert Farish
May, 1760,	John Moffett, James McDowell
August, 1760,	Sam. Wallace, Jr., Wm. Clark, John Peevie
September, 1760,	Thomas Stevenson, Richard Mays, Randal Lockhart
November 1, 1761,	William Ralston
November 17, 1761,	Daniel Harvey, Richard Morris
November 18, 1761,	David Caldwell, Moses Moore
November 21, 1761,	William Ward
December 29, 1761,	Adam Dunlop
January 11, 1762,	James Arbuckle
January 13, 1762,	James Kerr
January 18, 1762,	Edward Long
February 7, 1762,	James Moffet
February 16, 1762,	John Reaburn
February 17, 1762,	John Patterson
February 18, 1762,	John Carlile
February 25, 1762,	Sam. Cowdon
March 13, 1762,	Adam Thompson
March 18, 1762,	Robert Murphy
March 25, 1762,	James Hill
April 6, 1762,	Andrew Lockridge
April 17, 1762,	William Poage
April 23, 1762,	Robert Allen
April 27, 1762,	Thomas Poage
May 3, 1762,	James Robertson
May 4, 1762,	Thomas Nonyer, Drury Puckett
May 18, 1762,	Joseph Balckwood
May 25, 1762,	Andrew Russell
June 6, 1762,	Thomas Rafferty, Michael Coger, William Robinson
June 19, 1762,	Charles Lewis

July 20, 1762,	William Tees
August 18, 1762,	Robert Stuart, Robert Gorrell
September 13, 1762,	George Mathews
September 25, 1762,	James McAffee
September 30, 1762,	Samuel McMurty
October 17, 1765,	William McBride
November 4, 1765,	Robert Anderson
November 6, 1765,	Thomas Shanklin, Hugh Allen
May 21, 1766,	James Rodgers
May 23, 1766,	James Patterson
June 13, 1766,	Robert Campbell
June 20, 1766,	Pat. Christian
June 24, 1766,	John Taylor
August 20, 1766,	James Stewart
September 10, 1766,	Andrew Donelly
September 11, 1766,	Samuel Ralston
October 1, 1766,	Thomas Gaugh
November, 1767,	John Shanklin, Samuel Varner
April 29, 1768,	Robert Stevenson
July 6, 1768,	Henry King
July 20, 1768,	Thomas Bradshaw, Jr.
December 9, 1768,	Joseph Gamewell
January 16, 1769,	John Beard
March 21, 1769,	Alexander Reed, Jr.
May 11, 1769,	William Young
July 5, 1769,	John Wilson
July 10, 1769,	John Abney
August 28, 1769,	James Laird, Jr.
October 2, 1769,	Robert Gibson
October 11, 1769,	William Oldham
December 26, 1769,	William McClure
January 23, 1770,	Samuel Kilpatrick
January 24, 1770,	John McClenachan
April 10, 1770,	Pat. Buchanan
April 16, 1770,	Joseph Campbell
May 15, 1770,	Robert McClenachan, Jr.
June 9, 1770,	Abraham Lincoln
July 25, 1770,	Samuel Erwin
August 13, 1770,	Richard Woods
September 3, 1770,	John Patterson
October 3, 1770,	Matthew Kenny

October 16, 1770,	John Frogg
October 24, 1770,	Thomas Teese
December 5, 1770,	Pat. Lockhart
February 25, 1771,	Henry Hall
March 19, 1771, John Warwick, John McCreery,	Alexander Galesky
April 3, 1771,	John Craig
May 22, 1771,	Samuel Stevenson
May 29, 1771,	William Hamilton
July 14, 1771,	Thomas Smith
September 16, 1771,	William Trotter
December 10, 1771,	James Anderson
January 3, 1772,	John Harvie
February 21, 1772,	William Dunlop
March 12, 1772,	John Lewis
April 3, 1772,	James Curry
July 3, 1772,	Samuel Gibson
August 18, 1772,	James Craig
August 20, 1772,	Arch'd Dixon
November 27, 1772,	John Van Lear
November 30, 1772,	Thomas Posey
——————, 1772,	——— Alexander
February 2, 1773,	John Lewis
March 17, 1773,	Daniel Taylor
March 29, 1773,	James Trimble
May 8, 1773,	Solomon Estill
May 18, 1773,	James McClude
May 21, 1773,	William Hamilton
June 23, 1773,	William Sprowl

Lunenburg County

March 13, 1777,	John Cook and Elizabeth Cousins
July 4, 1786,	Richard Claiborne and Mary Cook
November 1, 1795,	Richard Kenner Cralle and Sarah Jones
August 4, 1788,	John Chappell and Martha Cross
December 9, 1773,	William Cowan and Mary Billups
November 8, 1770,	Charles Cross and Phebe Tomlinson
December 11, 1769,	William Grymes and Kesiah Dozer
December 8, 1775,	Bart Cox and ————

December 19, 1770, John Cureton and Sarah Moon, daughter of Gideon Moon.

November 10, 1763,	Theodrick Carter and Sally Ellbank
April 11, 1767,	Abraham Cocke and Agnes May
December 2, 1771,	John Cunningham and Mary Hill Pettipool
February 18, 1772,	John Chisholm and Elizabeth Muse
February 14, 1765,	Philip Goode and Anne Jones
November 8, 1764,	William Peasley and Lucy Sanders
February 15, 1775,	William Petterpoole and Frances Burk
September 27, 1775,	Frederick Nance and Susanna Christopher
February 13, 1778,	Lewis Page and Sally Justice
January 29, 1779,	William Pegram and Agnes Rhodes

March 26, 1779, Anthony Phillips and Lilian Binford. Letter of consent from parents, James and Mary Binford. She is of the age of twenty-one.

November 25, 1780, William Pennington and Drusilla Smithson. Letter from John and Drusilla Smithson, giving consent to marriage of their daughter Drusilla.

————, John Nash, Jr., and Anna Tabb Letter from Thomas Tabb father of Anna Tabb, saying the marriage was agreeable to him and to Col. Nash, father of John Nash, Jr.

February 9, 1768,	George Phillips and Ann Brown
August 10, 1775,	Isaac Oliver and Judah Bettes
March 12, 1785,	Nash Davis and ————

December 17, 1785, Ashley Davis and Mary Cross, daughter of John Cross.

December 14, 1780, Tscharner De Graffenreidt and Lucretia Robertson.

June 17, 1775,   Thomas Dozer and Catey Pryor

June, 1783, Metcalfe De Graffenreidt and Mary Ann Maury. Letter of consent from Abraham Maury for daughter Mary Ann.

—— 14, 1775,   William Dozer and Elizabeth Stokes

February 10, 1763, Tscharner De Graffenreidt and Elizabeth Embry

December 25, 1772, William De Graffenreidt and Elizabeth Robertson. Letter of consent from Thomas Robertson.

September 30, 1764, Robert Dixon and Anne Bacon. Consent of her father. Lyddall Bacon.

December 10, 1777,   James Crafton and Frances Staples

May 14, 1767,   William Crenshaw and Molly Haney

June 10, 1779,   William Carter and Mary Scott

January 26, 1779,   John Covington and Polly Williams

September 10, 1763, Thomas Egleton of Dinwiddie, and Anne Watson. Consent of Michael Watson, X his mark.

October 12, 1769, Ambrose Ellis and Sicily Stokes. Consent of Young Stokes, her father.

June 9, 1775, Martin Elam and Mary Philips, daughter of George Philips.

March 31, 1780,   Henry Embry and Ann Portes (?)

January 23, 1778,   John Estes and Mary Estes

February 1, 1780,   William Ellis and Sarah Briggs Chappell. Consent of father, Thomas Chappell.

February 3, 1778,   Seth Farley and Sarah Crafton

November 9, 1770, William Farley and Martha Farley. Consent of Henry Farley.

October 27, 1779,   Lodwick Farmer, Jr., and Elizabeth Herring

July 14, 1763,   James Foster and Susanna Wells, spinster

July 3, 1775,   Matthew Green and Ann Dowsing

March 24, 1792,   David Garland and Lucy Sturdivant.

September 8, 1796, James Garrett and Polly Johnson. Stephen Johnson's letter of consent.

October 13, 1785,   Edmund Gregory and Fanny Boswell

March 30, 1776,   Roger Gregory and Frances Lowry

January 28, 1765, Jeremiah Glenn and Anne Blagrave. Letter from Henry Blagrave, father of Anne.

July 12, 1770, John Glenn and Sarah Bacon. Letter of consent to daughter's marriage from Mary Smelt.

March 12, 1767,   Peter Garland and Martha Garland. David Garland's letter of consent to daughter's marriage.

July 2, 1764, David Garland's letter of consent to the marriage of George Jefferson and daughter Elizabeth Garland.

March 20, 1770,   Nathaniel Garrett and Eleanor Hight

Westmoreland County

August 30, 1786,   Richard Weaver and Elizabeth Carter
September 9, 1786,   Jeremiah Claxton and Molley Payton
December 27, 1786,   William Dishman and Elizabeth Monroe
January 24, 1778,   William Sanford and Ann Spence
October 31, 1786,   John Craighill and Elizabeth Hipkins
December 21, 1786,   William Anderson and Ann King
December 21, 1786,   Presley Neale and Sally Jackson
November 14, 1786,   William Crash and Frances Jenkins
December 12, 1786,   John Snow and Jemima Crabb
November 24, 1786,   John Butler and Mary Shoots
October 17, 1786,   Le Roy Daingerfield and Elizabeth Parker,
     Richard Parker, her father, gives his consent
December 13, 1786,   John Davis and Amy Griffis
October 26, 1786,   John Pilsbury and Sally Scott
September 23, 1786,   James Wigley and Jane Clark
November 23, 1786,   James Lawrence and Winnifred Ross
December 18, 1786,   Isaac Dade and Fanny Blundell
September 11, 1786,   William Butler and Alice Butler, Christo-
     pher Butler, her father, gives his consent.
July 27, 1793,   Richard Brinn and Elizabeth Anderson
October 7, 1786,   John Harrison and Issabel Jones
December 27, 1786,   James Payne and Ann Hunter
October 28, 1786,   George Rust and Elizabeth Dunbar
October 19, 1786,   Isaac Stone and Nancy Jett
October 30, 1786,   William Franklin and Ann Collinsworth
October 3, 1786,   James Sutton and Frances White
September 6, 1787,   George Turnbull and Sally Spence
April 9, 1787,   Edward Rogers Wright and Aggay Randall
June 20, 1787,   Francis Trigger and Ann Drake
June 12, 1787,   John Roe and Ann Monroe, Elizabeth Monroe, her
     mother, gives her consent
February 13, 1787,   John Hudnall and Elizabeth Jett, Thos. Hud-
     nall, his father, gives his consent

November 9, 1787,   Charles Gibbs and Nancy Williams

August 10, 1787,   James Richardson and Nancy Dishman, John
     Dishman, her father, gives his consent

January 21, 1787,   Richard Drake and Jane Thomson, John Thom-
     son, her father, gives his consent

October 10, 1787,   Thos. Clark and Jemima Scutt

September 27, 1781,   Travis Jones and Nancy Wright Davis

November 24, 1787,   Edward Sanford and Patty Yeatman

January 31, 1787,   Williams Franks and Elizabeth Sanford

January 31, 1787,   Edward Waller and Sally Callis

July 11, 1787,   Aaron Hardage and Sally Harrison

March 27, 1787,   Edmund Bulger and Hannah Corbit Hudson

October 22, 1787,   Joseph Moxley and Caty Clayton

December 25, 1787,   Weedon Arnold and Mary Morriss, Charles
     Morriss, her father, gives his consent

January 2, 1787,   George Courtney and Ann Jeffries, William Jef-
     fries, her father, gives his consent

January 26, 1787,   John Holt and Jane Balderson

January 13, 1787,   Kitchen Prim and Mary Clark

January 29, 1787,   Jeremiah Moxley and Hannah Morriss

July 7, 1787,   John Francis Gaullier and Elizabeth Sanders

January 16, 1787,   Gerrard Hutt and Ann Robinson

October 15, 1787,   James Berryman and Margaret Sthreshley

June 15, 1787,   Griffin Jones and Sarah Boyd

June 7, 1787,   Thomas Hill and Martha Pierce

March 9, 1787,   John Mathany and Winny Barecroft,

March 2, 1787,   William Dodd and Heniritta Weaver

March 17, 1787,   Thomas D. Downing and Bettsy Cox

April 11, 1787,   Eskridge Hall and Sevina Jenkins

September 29, 1787,   James Fegens and Molly Self

November 8, 1787,   John Murphy and Anne Ballantine, John Bal-
     lantine, her father, gives his consent

November 17, 1787,   John Elmore and Elander Cluskey

November 12, 1787,   John Barnett and Hannah Curtis, Rebecka
     Curtis, her mother, gives her consent

December 1, 1787,   Bennett W. Guy and Hannah Eckles

August 22, 1787,   John Wood and Molly Cahall

July 26, 1787,   John Tupman and Patsy Thomas

February 3, 1787,   Richard Caddeen and Mary Bennett

February 27, 1787,   John Pillion and Clowey Allison

April 30, 1787,   William Craghill and Charlott Hipkins

February 15, 1787,   Spencer Johnson and Hannah Williams
February 5, 1787,   John Bowen and Rachell Drake, Rose Drake, her mother, gives her consent
December 21, 1787,   Opie Lindsay and Frankey Jett
November 7, 1787   John Potter and Margaret Hawkins
October 30, 1787,   Jesse Bennett and Jemima Cole
July 18, 1787,   Richard Wintfield and Mary Lawrence
February 7, 1787,   John Kew and Jane Payton
May 8, 1787,   Corbin Washington and Hannah Lee
December 3, 1787,   Thomas Butler and Frances Moxley, Joseph Moxley and Frances Moxley, her parents, give their consent
July 13, 1787,   Gerrard Garner and Nancy Hull, George Hull and Letty Hull, her parents, give their consent
January 1, 1787,   William White and Sarah Kitchen
December 30, 1790,   Lawrence Pope and Frances Carter
December 3, 1790,   Rev. William Edwards and Franky Pope, Lars Pope, her father, gives his consent
April 9, 1790,   John Kirk and Elender McKenney
November 30, 1790,   Abner Howe and Nancy Harrison, Wm. Harrison, her father, gives his consent
January 23, 1790,   Thomas Annadale and Penny Mothershead
July 31, 1790,   William Palmer and Peggy Sanford
January 30, 1790,   James A. Thompson and Rebecca Newton Jackson, Rebecca Jackson, her mother, gives her consent
March 18, 1790,   Col. Alexander Parker and Elizabeth Redman
May 20, 1788,   Robert Fergusson and Elizabeth Ballantine, John Ballantine, her father, gives his consent
December 1, 1788,   Robert Anthony and Lettice Gregory, Lettice Gregory and James Gregory, her parents, give their consent
March 29, 1788,   David Annadale and Winefred Clayton
January 10, 1788,   Burwell Bassett and Eliza McCarty, Dan'l McCarty, her father, gives his consent
October 13, 1788,   Thomas Lee, Sr., and Mildred Washington, Hannah Washington, her mother, gives her consent
May 16, 1788,   Thomas Washington and Sarah Harper
January 22, 1788,   Ludwell Lee and Flora Lee
April 29, 1788,   John Woollard and Jemima Redman
June 7, 1788,   Winder Nash and Sally Alverson
May 6, 1788,   George Bailey Smith and Ann Deatterly
March 22, 1788,   John Beane and Ann King

March 26, 1788,   Spencer Ball and Betsy Landon Carter, Robt.
   Carter, her father, gives his consent
February 4, 1788,   William Murdock and Nancy Berton
March 6, 1788,   George Hill and Roseannah Brinnon, Roseannah
   Brinnon, her mother, gives her consent
February 12, 1788,   James Bland and Ursula Gordon
March 22, 1788,   James Deatterly and Elizabeth Fegitt
December 30, 1788,   John Lyell and Sarah Robinson
February 26, 1788,   Alexander Young and Nancy Green, Margaret
   Green,her mother, gives her consent
December 23, 1788,   Richard Bennett and Alice Middleton, George
   Middleton, her father, gives his consent
May 27, 1788,   William Porter and Mary Sandy, Uriah Sandy and
   Anne Sandy, her parents, give their consent
January 17, 1788,   Doctor John Goldsmith and Julia Arnold alias
   Lovell, John Lovell, her father, gives his consent
October 16, 1788,   Richard Bruer and Ann Blackwell, Thos. Down-
   ing, her guardian, gives his consent
May 13, 1788,   John Piper and Jenny Fox, Jos. Fox, her father,
   gives his consent.
April 30, 1788,   John Templeman and Ellen Lawson
January 29, 1788,   John Middleton and Hannah Wroe
September 17, 1788,   Obediah Mors and Ann Self
December 8, 1788,   John Stewart and Ann Carmichael
December 15, 1788,   Thomas Spence and Caty Sanford alias Caty
   Pope.
January 31, 1788,   John Brown Steel and Sarah Collinsworth
February 26, 1788,   Thos. Worth and Nelly Drake
January 18, 1788,   John Coleman and Susannah Critcher
December 23, 1788,   James Edmunds and Molley Cook
September 6, 1788,   William Self and Jemima Partridge
December 19, 1788,   Thomas Colebeck and Matilda Garner
April 5, 1788,   Joseph Fox and Mary Hipkins
January 11, 1788,   Richard Baker and Sarah Roe
January 2, 1788,   Thomas Stone and Alice Bruer
December 8, 1789,   John Ball and Anna Thomas
December 16, 1789,   William Sisson and Peggy Muse, Susanna
   Muse, her mother, gives her consent
January 8, 1789,   Robert Sanford and Sally Newton
October 3, 1789,   Daniel Crabb and Frances Middleton
January 7, 1789,   Edward Porter and Mary McClanaham

November 13, 1789,   John Billins and Elizabeth Reynolds
September 29, 1789,   Henry Thomson and Catharine McGuy
June 5, 1789,   William Walker Short and Ann Smith
October 23, 1789, Thomas Short and Mary Ann Brown, Ann
    Owen, her mother, gives her consent
October 21, 1789, Charles Sanders and Elizabeth Watson, Martha
    Sanders and Susanar Sanders, his parents, give their consent
October 19, 1789,   Thomas Williams and Sarah Hodge
September 15, 1789, William Drake and Ann Payton, Mary But-
    ler, her mother, gives her consent
June 2, 1789,   James Roles and Molley Robinson, Sarah Robinson
    her mother, gives her consent
March 23, 1789,   Thomas Sutton and Nancy Robinson
November 11, 1789,   Teliff Alverson and Alice Brinham
October 26, 1789,   William Collinsworth and Nancy Caddean
May 27, 1789,   John Wood and Ann Price
November 24, 1789, Josiah Sutton and Elizabeth Davis, Elias
    Davis, her father, gives his consent
January 1, 1789,   James Rice and Jemima Spence
July 7, 1789,   Charles Oliff and Franky Davis Green
January 27, 1789,   William Packett and Ann Cooper
February 10, 1789,   Charles Wickliff and Susannah Nelson
December 28, 1789,   Peter Smith and Sarah Smith, Moses Self,
    her guardian, gives his consent
December 26, 1789,   Youel Self and Ann Walker
December 30, 1789,   David Wardrobe and Elen Garner
        1789,   Daniel Crabb and Frances Burgess Smith
April 28, 1789,   Samuel Green and Elizabeth Edwards
April 2, 1789, George Moore and Mary Sutton, Richard Sutton.
    her father, gives his consent
January 13, 1789, Alexander Moxley and Nancy Quisenbury,
    Nicho. Quisenbury, her father, gives his consent
August 31, 1789,   Matthew Bayne and Caty Harrison
March 6, 1789,   Richard Sutton and Fanny Chilton Marmaduke
March 17, 1789,   John McKenny and Peggy Sutton
March 16, 1789,   Richard Moxley and Salley Sisson
March 24, 1789,   Reuben Cannaday and Easter Green
March 10, 1789,   John Jett and Frances James
December 2, 1789, James Fegitt and Molley Jones, William Jones,
    her father, gives his consent
January 24, 1789,   John Howell and Sally Gregory

March 29, 1789,   Benedict Lamkin and Molley King
September 22, 1789,   George Deatley and Sally Mothershead
April 10, 1789,   Rodham Blancett and Jane Brown
April 14, 1789,   George Oliff and Mary Landoram
December 9, 1789,   John Eskridge and Elizabeth Moxley
April 7, 1789,   Seth Starr and Elizabeth Lawson Eskridge
August 7, 1793, Austin Pope and Fanny Yeatman, Thos. Yeat-
    man, her father, gives his consent
November 22, 1793,   Lawrence Pope and Peney Vigar
June 29, 1793, Bernard Jackson and Sally Claxton, Jerimiah
    Claxton, her father, gives his consent
October 9, 1793,   Thomas Beane and Elizabeth Redeck
November 12, 1793, John Robinson and Elizabeth Davis, Elias
    Davis, her father, gives his consent
January 7, 1793,   Lovell Bryan and Elizabeth Weedon
January 2, 1793,   James Drake and Jenny Jones
January 2, 1793,   Stephen Craine and Cloey Hewlet
January 11, 1793,   Spencer Ball and Elizabeth Thomas, James
    Thomas, her father, gives his consent
February 20, 1793,   Christopher Jackson and Rockey Holland
December 28 1793   Vincent Bramham and Hannah Bushrod Smith
July 22, 1793,   John Grisset and Ann Pursley, Mary Wells, her
    mother, gives her consent
July 19, 1793,   James Hawkins and Mary Reynolds
July 23, 1793,   William Bruer and Magdalin Lewis
August 19, 1793,   Jesse Gouldin and Peggy Moxley
August 30, 1793,   Thomas Figgat and Matilday Coleback
May 28, 1793,   Landman Short and Susannah Tait
July 9, 1793,   William W. Smith and Betsy Monroe, David Monroe,
    her father, gives his consent
December 24, 1793,   William Sherley and Cloe Merchant
May 7, 1793,   Thomas Maddox and Jane Middleton Crabb, John
    Crabb, her father, gives his consent
August 27, 1793,   Samuel Crabb and Mary Middleton
December 11, 1793,   William Scrimsher and Frances Sanford
December 28, 1793, Peter Rust and Elizabeth Ball Downman,
    John Claughton, her guardian, gives her consent
January 15, 1794,   Chas. Bell and Winifred C. Rust
July 3, 1793,   Lewis Chastain and Elizabeth Rust
June 25, 1793,   Alex. Harrison and Alice Nelson
November 26, 1793,   Thos. Jett and Peggy Berkley

July 12, 1793,   John Barrick and Mary Brann

March 18, 1793,   James Harvey and Lucette Fox, Jo. Fox, her father, gives his consent

July 18, 1793,   Thomas Stowers and Keziah Robinson

April 4, 1793,   Nathaniel Oldham and Martha Middleton

April 30, 1793,   George Lewis and Hannah Thomas

December 30, 1793,   William Gilbert and Elinor Porter, Demcey Porter, her father, gives his consent

April 2, 1793,   Tarpley Bryant and Sarah Bariott, John Bariott, her father, gives his consent

December 19, 1793,   Francis Jett and Sally Sims, Elizabeth Sims (?), her mother, gives her consent

March 26, 1793,   Robert Massey and Molley Jett

November 23, 1793,   Samuel Johnson and Sarah Hinson, Joshu Hinson, her father, gives his consent

March 22, 1793,   Benjamin McKenny and Molley McKenny

September 24, 1793,   Thos. Mozingo and Mary Cannaday

January 15, 1793,   William Sanders and Mary Peed

June 14, 1793,   Dozier T. Cavender and Elizabeth Gill

March 9, 1793,   William Stone and Peggy Morriss, Charles Morriss, her father, gives his consent

December 24, 1793,   Allen Ashton and Elizabeth Lucas

December 24, 1793,   William Reynolds and Hannah Morton

November 26, 1793,   William Hunter and Fanny Marmaduke

June 3, 1793,   John Rochester and Ann McClanaham

December 31, 1793,   Lawson Moore and Betsy Rochester

March 24, 1790,   Matthew Partridge and Elizabeth Bathen Self

March 31, 1790,   George Garner and Anne Middleton

January 26, 1790,   Anthony Payton and Betsy Hudwall

May 15, 1790,   Samuel Johnson and Elizabeth Cannaday

December 22, 1790,   John Penstone and Martha Bragg, Elizabeth Bragg, her mother, gives her consent

November 2, 1790,   James Dodd and Patty Massey, Elizabeth Massey, her mother, gives her consent

December 30, 1790,   David Ashton and Nancy Bowden, Nancy Bowden, her mother, gives her consent

December 11, 1790,   Patrick Lynch and Deliby Dodd

December 21, 1790,   Richard Carter and Susannah Briscoe

December 4, 1790,   Jesse Butler and Sally Stott, Robert Stott, her father, gives his consent

December 10, 1790,   James Brewer and Betsey Turnbull

October 28, 1790, Henry Gutridge and Sally Sneed Morton
August 31, 1790, James Butler and Elizabeth Barecroft
January 7, 1790, Ozmond Crabbe and Winifred Hartly
January 12, 1790, James M. Guy and Molley Collins
August 5, 1790, Andrew Cohoon and Prissilley Weaver, An. Weaver, her father, gives his consent
September 22, 1790, Thomas Steel and Jemima Barkley
October 6, 1790, John Short and Anne Owens
September 29, 1790, Jacob Johnston and Betsy Nelson, Wills Nelson and Susanna Nelson, her parents, give their consent
November 9, 1790, Walker Muse and Susanna Muse
September 18, 1790, John Neale and Elizabeth Brewer
July 7, 1790, John Harper and Hannah Harrison Waumoths
May 20, 1790, Samuel Harrison and Patty S. Harper
May 15, 1790, Thomas Hodge and Caty Washington
October 21, 1790, Gerard B. Berryman and Alice Quisenbury, George Robinson and Elizabeth Robinson, her parents, give their consent
January 12, 1790, Smith King and Jane Middleton Self, Henry Self, her father, gives his consent
May 25, 1790, William Weathers Spoon and Joyce Butler
June 9, 1790, James Hore and Frances Nelson
June 3, 1790, John Collinsworth and Sebinah Weaver
June 14, 1790, John Feggitt and Nancy Mullins
June 29, 1790, Reuben Briscoe and Betsy Thorp
October 23, 1790, John Jenkins and Elizabeth Mothershead
December 6, 1790, James Roy and Nancy Washington, Const. Washington, her mother, gives her consent
December 28, 1791, William Hazard and Mary Shadrack
December 27, 1791, John McClanaham and Mary Robinson, Solomon Robinson, her father, gives his consent
December 20, 1791, William Mooklar and Sally Atwell, Mary Atwell, her mother, gives her consent
December 24, 1791, John Dodd and Elizabeth Sanford
July 29, 1791, George McKenney and Elizabeth McGuire
August 19, 1791, William McKenney and Frances McKenney
December 7, 1791, Gerard McKenney and Peggy Templeman
December 27, 1791, James Hart and Peggy Muse, Rich'd Muse, her father, gives his consent
August 31, 1791, William Nelson and Mary Harrison
February 22, 1791, Zachariah Alverson and Keziah Burgess

March 7, 1791, William Griggs and Hannah Self, Margaret Self,
    her mother, gives her consent
August 30, 1791,   Thomas Gregory and Precilliar McKenney
November 18, 1791,   Edmund Denny and Betsy Triplett
September 27, 1791,   John Tippit and Mary Clark
August 20, 1791,   John Hughs and Winefrit Hawood
July 10, 1791,   James Spark and Harnar Parker
July 5, 1791,   Nathaniel Nash and Darcus Fryer
January 25, 1791,   William Stone and Sarah Morriss
January 25, 1791,   John Hinson and Molly Deane
January 5, 1791,   John Locust and Sarah Kelly
January 31, 1791, Henry Barnett and Alleymenty Carroll, John
    Carroll, her father, gives his consent
May 13, 1791,   Samuel Smith and Elizabeth Harrison
November 23, 1791,   Thomas Cook and Sally Hullums
December 19, 1791,   Ebenezer Balderson and Anne Clark
December, 23, 1793,   Rodam McGuy and Mary Askins
May 31, 1791,   Nathaniel Lucas and Nelly Lawrence
December 16, 1793,   Saml. Efford and Elizabeth Doleman
December 29, 1791,   Samuel Beale and Susannah Smith
July 23, 1791,   Edward Hall and Betsey McGuy
December 27, 1791,   John Courtney and Elizabeth Mors
June 7, 1791,   John Weaver and Mary Williams
May 21, 1791,   John Mathany and Mary Jeffriess
May 10, 1791,   Jesse Yeatman and Jenny Brown
April 2, 1791,   Jeremiah Edmonds and Martha Carter
April 22, 1791, William S. Hutchings and Nancy, Thomas Caven-
    der, her father, gives his consent, and John Hutchings, his
    father, gives his consent
May 2, 1791,   Warner Bashaw and Aggatha Wright
November 19, 1791,   Thomas Muse and Elizabeth Sanford
February 12, 1791,   George Middleton and Martha Attwell
February 15, 1791,   William Davis and Anne Worth
March 2, 1791 John Green Johnson and Nancy Bettisworth, John
    Bettisworth, her father, gives his consent
March 7, 1791,   Campbell Robinson Teet and Peggy Edsir Cole
December 19, 1791,   Orrick Chilton and Felicia Corbin
January 22, 1791,   Lovell Peirce and Patty Moxley
January 4, 1791,   George Wills and Prudence Bowden
July 26, 1791,   Thos. Newman and Peggy Jett Bartlet
April 15, 1791,   Newman Hammon and Agatha Lucas

March 29, 1791,   John Hennage and Delila James
January 27, 1791,   Nicholas Muse and Anne Thompson
August 29, 1791,   John S. Sutton and Rebecca Eskridge
June 24, 1791,   Samuel Muse and Mary Arnol
March 19, 1792, John Underwood and Molly Muse, Richd. Muse,
    her father, gives his consent
December 29, 1792,   Richard Mothershead and Margarett Muse
January 20, 1792,   Benedict Wright and Mary Rust, Vincent Rust,
    her father gives his consent
December 5, 1792,   Smith Jenkins and Jemima Washington
June 16, 1792,   John Muse and Tabitha Gardner
September, 5, 1792,   William Pope and Penny Annadale
November 8, 1792,   William Furlong Colvin and Agathy Wright
October 27, 1792,   Youel Brinnon and Sarah McKenney
November, 17, 1792, Thomas Attwell and Molley Spence Griggs,
    Henry Griggs, her father, gives his consent
December 19, 1792,   John Turberville and Anne Ballantine
September 4, 1792,   Thomas Hutt and Mary Sturman
July 4, 1792, William A. Washington and Mary Lee, Richard Henry
    Lee, her father, gives his consent
July 30, 1792,   Andrew Harriss and Anne Hall
July 14, 1792, John Burges and Frances James Pitman, Joseph
    Burges, his father, gives his consent
October, 9, 1792,   Daniel Boyer and Elizabeth Fegins
August 25, 1792,   George Gregory and Ann Fitzgerrald, John
    Fitzgerrald and Lidy Fitzgerrald, her parents, give their con-
    sent
December 18, 1792,   Thomas Coleman and Hannah Boyer
December 15, 1792,   John Rose and Nancy Lamkin
December 19, 1792,   James Jewell and Moley Martin
September 11, 1792,   Stephen Moore and Sally Butler
March 27, 1792, Richd. Clark and Sarah Cooper, Jas. Triplett,
    guardian, gives his consent
May 28, 1792, Charles Sanford and Betty Porter, Charles Sanford,
    his father, gives his consent
October 9, 1792,   Reuben Briant and Nancy Iles
November 5, 1793,   Jeremiah Garner and Deborah Mors
September 25, 1792,   Reuben Moore and Charlotte Thomas
December 3, 1792,   James Brewer and Betsy Spence
June 26, 1792, Johnson Wright and Polly Dawson, W. Dawson,
    her father, gives his consent

April 8, 1795,   John Evin and Judy Tate
September 18, 1792,   Benedict Middleton and Hannah Harrison
January 21, 1792,   James Pegg and Elizabeth Hallbrooks
November 20, 1792, Rev. James Elliott and Elizabeth Brocken-
    brough, Austin Brockenbrough, her father, gives his consent
September 14, 1792,   Peter Davis and Patty McGuire
January 3, 1792,   James Spurling and Charlotte Carpenter
March 24, 1792,   John Weaver and Penny Sanford
March 16, 1792,   Thomas Sandy and Anne Lewis
May 12, 1792,   Charles Chrisman and Bethlehem Rose
April 24, 1792,   Nathaniel King and Elizabeth Dishman
June 22, 1792,   John Critcher and Lettice Garner
June 21, 1792,   Thomas Morse and Ann Sisson
June 20, 1792, John Asbury and Patty Self, Stephen Self, her
    father, gives his consent
January 21, 1792, Charles R. Thompson and Mary Jackson, Re-
    becca Jackson, her mother, gives her consent
October 9, 1792,   Samuel Beale and Alice Harris
January, 31, 1792, Benjamin Hammock and Patty Scutt, Charles
    Scutt, her father, gives his consent
March 3, 1792,   Randall Kirk and Elizabeth Brinn
February 28, 1792,   Samuel Berryman and Ann Berkley
November 7, 1792,   James King and Ellender Anderson
February 22, 1794,   Jonathan Rigg and Catharine Quisenbury,
    Nichs. Quisenbury, her father, gives his consent
December 16, 1794,   James Green and Susannah Dunton
November 10, 1794,   James Grant and Sarah Lambert
March 15, 1794,   John Brown and Ann Spence
August 14, 1794, John Nash and Molley Reynolds, James Nash,
    his father, gives his consent
October 14, 1794,   William Nash and Elizabeth Spilman, Anne
    Spilman, her mother, gives her consent
June 18, 1794,   William S. Hutt and Constance U. E. Villard
May 12, 1794,   Joseph Thompson and Judith B. Rowand
June 14, 1794, John Mullins and Ruthey Barret, Elizabeth Jones,
    her mother, gives her consent
December 13, 1794, Richard Lee Turberville and Henneritta Lee,
    Anne Lee, her mother, gives her consent
September 20, 1794, Reuben G. Sutton and Sarah Ann Mullins
May 21, 1794, John Feagitt and Caty Self, Presley Self, her
    father, gives his consent

July 16, 1794, George Barnwell Carey and Winnefred Garner, James Garner, her father, gives his consent

August 26, 1794, David Annadale and Mary Poor, Charles Poor, her father, gives his consent

September 23, 1794, Jeremiah Leacock and Elizabeth Kenner

January 18, 1794, Daniel Mathany and Patty McClanaham

January 27, 1794, William L. Davis and Elizabeth H. King, Peter Davis, his father, gives his consent

January 20, 1794, John Carr and Sarah Bruce

April 22, 1794, Bennett Baxter and Ann Robinson Jones, Thomas Jones, her father, gives his consent

February 12, 1794, George Curtis and Molly Douglass

January 28, 1794, William Turner and Nanny Conkling

March 25, 1794, Andrew Balmain and Nancy C. Ray

December 3, 1794, Thomas Sorrell and Elizabeth Lucass, John Lucass, her father, gives his consent

January 15, 1794, Thomas Bell and Hannah Rust, Ann Rust, her mother, gives her consent

September 22, 1794, Richard Read and Betsy Washington

January 26, 1795, John Parker and Elizabeth Muse, Richard Muse, guardian to E. Muse, gives his consent

January 21, 1795, Benjamin Steel and Ellen Deatterly

August 31, 1795, Bodington Frank and Mary Beane

April 10, 1795, John Porter and Patty Sisson

April 17, 1795, John Turner and Susanna Butler

April 10, 1795, John C. Self and Deborah Garner

April 25, 1795, William Luttrell and Elizabeth Marmaduke

April 16, 1795, John Morriss and Elizabeth McKave

January 15, 1795, Jeremiah Blundell and Ann Pomroy, Jacob Pomroy, her father, gives his consent

January 15, 1795, John Grinnan and Jane Clarke, Jane Wigley and James Wigley, her parents, give their consent

January 14, 1795, Richard Luttrell and Elizabeth Ellmore

August 1, 1795, Elliott Monroe and Susannah Davis

August 11, 1795, Richard Sanford and Hannah Sutton

July 16, 1795, Anthony A. Harrison and Hannah Sanford

June 22, 1795, Robert Carter and Nancy Spilman

August 24, 1795, Daniel Crabb and Ann Gill

November 19, 1795, Doctor Henry Rose and Ann Washington Robinson, John Rose, her guardian, gives his consent

December 8, 1795, Reuben Bailey and Mary Sutton, Nancy Sutton, her mother, gives her consent
May 15, 1795, Marmaduke Brockenbrough Beckwith and Rebecca Beckwith
August 29, 1795, Samuel Thrift and Ann Self
September 18, 1795, John Brown and Margaret Self
January 27, 1795, Samuel Beale and Nancy Garner, James Garner, her father, gives his consent
December 30, 1795, Fleet Lamkin and Charlotte Settle
December 7, 1795, Lee Pittman and Lottey Garner
August 26, 1795, Nathen Spriggs and Elizabeth C. Brinnon
December 28, 1795, Joel S. Rose and Frances Weaver, Corbin Washington, her guardian, gives his consent
September 10, 1795, Thomas Thorpe and Elizabeth Butler, Christopher Butler, her father, gives his consent
October 12, 1795, John Rose and Sebinah Collinsworth
November 18, 1795, George Daniel and Hannah King
March 24, 1795, Champ Brockenbrough and Sally Skinker Bowie, Sarah Bowie, her mother, gives her consent
February 24, 1795, William Redman and Elizabeth Shoats
March 7, 1795, Thomas Plummer and Moley Middleton
November 23, 1795, Robert Gibson and Margaret Mazarett
January 21, 1795, Thomas Yeatman and Elizabeth McClanaham
May 14, 1796, Thomas R. Robinson and Jemima Mathews
December 30, 1795, William Fobes and Hannah Gordon
December 29, 1795, Youell Davis and Caty Preits
May 23, 1796, Willoughby Newton and Sally Lee
September 3, 1796, Pemberton Claughton and Sally Neale, William Claughton, guardian, gives his consent
January 4, 1796, John Butler and Mary Muse
October 18, 1796, Peter Presley Cox and Fanny Bailey
November 1, 1796, Robert S. Hipkins and Mary H. Butler, Beckwith Butler, her father, gives his consent
December 7, 1796, William Hazard and Ann Blundell
November 28, 1796, Thomas Lyne and Susannah Morriss, Charles Morriss, her father, gives his consent
April 20, 1796, Hugh Quintan and Anne Tasker Peck
December 6. 1796, Samuel Bruer and Alice Sanders, Ailsey Sanders and Joseph Sanders, her parents, give their consent
January 22, 1796, John Davis and Betsy Dolman, James McNeil her guardian, gives his consent

November 28, 1796, Benjamin P. Weeks and Mary Smith, Lusetta
  Smith, her mother, gives her consent
June 22, 1796, David Ashton and Betty Newgent
June 3, 1796, Robert McKildoe and Bettey Sanford
September 2, 1796, Thomas Short and Peggy Gregory, John Gregory, her father, gives his consent
August 25, 1796, Presley Stone and Fanny Baker Blundell
October 12, 1796, John Garner and Nancy Angel
October 10, 1796, William Nelson and Jane Martin, Jacob Martin, her father, gives his consent
April 5, 1796, Francis Attwell and Fanny McCave
April 8, 1796, Elijah Weaver and Elizabeth Frary
November 28, 1796, John Bryant and Frances Brawner
December 12, 1796, Campbell R. Teet and Elizabeth Mothershead
January 7, 1796, Edward Stone and Jemima Sanford, Thomas
  Sanford, her father, gives his consent
December 14, 1796, William Doleman and Ammaly Montgomery
January 4, 1796, William Williams and Alice Cannady
December 8, 1796, John Lyell and Lucy Sanford, Charles Sanford, her father, gives his consent
December 20, 1796, Baldwin B. Smith and Elizabeth Jackson
December 28, 1796, John Sanford and Dianna McKenny, Gerard
  McKenny, her guardian, gives his consent
February 22, 1796, John B. Jenkins and Martha A. Omolumdro
June 3, 1796, Hudson Purcelley and Fanny Mothershead
June 18, 1796, Thomas Ennis and Caty Carpenter
May 28, 1796, James Clark and Pennelope Sanford, Reuben Sanford, her father, gives his consent
May 28, 1796, Augustine Sanford and Jemima Hazard
March 4, 1796, Daniel Burgess and Mary Wood
March 23, 1796, Richard Thompson and Jane Nelson, William
  Nelson gives his consent
January 12, 1796, James Butler and Elizabeth Beale, Nancy Beale, her mother, gives her consent
May 19, 1795, Thomas Pursley and Elizabeth Riels
May 23, 1796, Jeremiah Moxley and Hannah Robinson
May 10, 1796, Richard Mozingo and Nancy Yardly
April 13, 1796, William Greenlaw and Sally R. Peirce, Jos. Peirce, her father, gives his consent
April 9, 1796, Henry Asbury and Sally Moxley
December 21, 1797, Thos. William Clark and Frances Wroe

December 21, 1797, John Peede and Jenny Guttridge, Thomas Guttridge, her father, gives his consent

October 13, 1797,   Vincent Reynolds and Winney Brickey

December 23, 1797,   Richard Ashton and Jenny Lawrence

December 28, 1797, Joseph Mounett and Jane Owen, Ann Owen, her mother, gives her consent

September 27, 1797,   Bennett Rose and Elizabeth Hutchings

Sptember 19, 1797,   John Carter and Mary Carter

February 9, 1797, Reuben Jordon and Amelia P. Hall, Elisher Hall, her father, gives his consent

September 11, 1797,   John Muse and Caty Davis

December 28, 1797,   Joseph Taite and Felitia Ashton

December 29, 1797,   Nathaniel Collinsworth and Nancy Garner

June 5, 1797,   Edward Burn and Nancy Carpenter

May 22, 1797,   Richard Walker and Mary P. Morgan

July 24, 1797,   James Booth and Susannah Crenshaw

September 2, 1797, Dan'l. McCarty and Margaret Robinson, John Rose, her guardian, gives his consent

July 31, 1797,   Presley McKenny and Nancy McKenny

May 22, 1797,   Daniel Sanford and Susannah Sanders

November 15, 1797, Stephen Bailey and Ellen Templeman, John Templeman and Ellen Templeman, her parents, give their consent

January 12, 1797,   William McKenny and Caty Sanford

November 29, 1797, James Hackney and Caty Muse, Walk. Muse, her father, gives his consent

November 6, 1797,   George Woosencroft and Mary Self

November 4, 1797,   Martin Sisson and Caty Moxley

June 24, 1797,   Newton Hails and Sarah Rose

June 26, 1797,   George Sisson and Mary S. Redman

January 23, 1797,   Samuel Walker and Anne Montgomery

July 13, 1797,   Reuben Gutriddge and Elizabeth Carter

February 13, 1797,   Thomas Eskridge and Winefred Eyles

January 23, 1797,   Syms C. Glascock and Elizabeth Middleton

November 18, 1797, William Hammock and Betsy Pursely, Mary Pursely, her mother, gives her consent

December 6, 1797,   George B. Smith and Martha Attwell

December 6, 1797, Dawson G. Toombs and Mary Kelsick, Hugh McNeil, her guardian, gives his consent

July 4, 1797,   John Gregory and Nancy Williams

February 1, 1797, Robert Sanford and Aggay Hazard, William
    Hazard, her father, gives his consent
May 12, 1797,   James Bland and Alice Barnett
February 11, 1797,   Reuben Brann and Frances Garlick
June 27, 1797,   William Wroe and Sarah Carter
February 17, 1797, Jonathan Grimes and Hannah Mann, Jane
    Mann, her mother, gives her consent
February 24, 1797,   George Longworth and Molley Landman
March 13, 1797,   Solomon Robinson and Frances Redman
February 27, 1797,   Henry Franks and Franky Sanford
January 10, 1797, John Monroe and Betsy Triplett, Jas. Triplett,
    her father, gives his consent
April 18, 1797,   John D. Oliff and Rebecca Scott
January 31, 1797,   Sampson Marmaduke and Mary Ann Jones
January 31, 1797,   William Omohundro and Nancy Marmaduke
February 25, 1797,   William Marmaduke and Martha Clark
June 26, 1797,   John Crabb and Essey Rochester
January 4, 1797,   Benedict Rust and Elizabeth Middleton
June 9, 1798,   Samuel Beale and Judah Middleton
August 8, 1798, William Settle and Mary Greenlaw, William
    Greenlaw, her father, gives his consent
May 31, 1798,   Robert Annedale and Mary Good
June 16, 1798,   Vincent Edmund and Frances Balderson
May 26, 1798,   Frances Bevetton and Mary Lewis
February 21, 1798,   William Robertson and Elizabeth Jeffrice
February 13, 1798, William Hilton and Hannah Christopher Stott
July 28, 1798,   Jeremiah Stephens and Winefred Willson
January 17, 1798, Thomas Claxton and Alice Weaver, Susannah
    Weaver, her sister, gives her consent
September 24, 1798, Vincent McKenney and Jane Wilda Edwards
September 22, 1798,   William Walker and Elizabeth Hugh
July 31, 1798,   James Hinson and Nanny Marks
March 6, 1798,   Spencer Garner and Alice Bailey Washington
December 25, 1798,   James Smith and Elizabeth Thrilkell
April 11, 1798,   William Beddo and Fanny Hennage
February 21, 1798,   Samuel Rust and Sary Clanahan
December 4, 1798,   William Weaver and Elizabeth Collins
August 7, 1798,   James Guttridge and Elizabeth Morton
December 4, 1798,   John Ellmore and Nancy Hall
April 27, 1798,   Isaac Brinnon and Margaret Young
August 22, 1798,   Thomas Sanford and Frances Brown

June 25, 1798, Richard Thompson and Sally Yeatman, Thos. Yeatman, her father, gives his consent

May 16, 1798, Jesse Green and Lucetty Green, Sarah Green, her
mother, gives her consent

December 14, 1798,	Griffin G. Garner and Mary Griggs
Jun 22, 1798,	John Barker and Margaret Quisenbury
February 15, 1798,	John Carter and Sary Brewer
December 18, 1798,	James Payne and Anne Neale
September 11, 1798,	Rodham Hudson and Molley Dolman
February 26, 1798,	Epaphroditus Bashaw and Ann Robinson
December 24, 1798,	John King and Alice Wroe

September 19, 1798, John Payton and Mary Weeks, Tho. Hill, her
guardian, gives his consent

October 22, 1798,	George Scurlock and Milly Self
November 24, 1798,	Thomas Robinson and Kesiah Leader
November 28, 1798,	John Morton and Caty Mothershead

December 28, 1798, Martin Marrow and Elizabeth Kirk, John
Kirk, her father, gives his consent

January 31, 1798,	Joseph Marmaduke and Judith Stone
November 3, 1798,	Benjamin Rogers and Susannah Weaver
February 20, 1798,	James N. Rust and Peggy Courtney
December 30, 1799,	George Short and Frances Canadey
August 7, 1799,	Thomas Wilkerson and Sally Nelson
December 24, 1799,	Gerard McKenny and Frances Sutton

May 11, 1799, Solomon Redman and Frances Robinson, Solomon
Robinson, her father, gives his consent

March 23, 1799,   Jeremiah Claxton and Frances Sanford

February 6, 1799, Thomas Davis and Sally Drake, Rose Drake,
her mother, gives her consent

June 14, 1799,	Henry Beale and Darcus Garner
March 23, 1799,	William Spurling and Nancy Cary
January 23, 1799,	Reuben Garner and Ann Tupman
August 12, 1799,	Joseph Annadale and Jenne Carter
July 12, 1799,	Mourning Richardson and Byron Triplett
February 1, 1799,	Thomas Teet and Mary Robinson
March 25, 1799,	John White and Elisha Mothershead
May 27, 1799,	William S. Sanford and Elizabeth Yeatman
September 7, 1799,	William Palmer and Rockey Jackson
December 30, 1799,	James S. Mothershead and Elizabeth Riley

October 26, 1799, George Mothershead and Susey Green, Charles
Green and Marean Green, her parents, give their consent

June 3, 1799,   William Hutching and Frankey Curtis
December 11, 1799,   Reubin Sanford and Anne Washington
June 11, 1799,   George Woosencroft and Sally Jenkins
June 10, 1799, William A. Hipkins and Margaret Martin, Jacob
    Martin, her father, gives his consent
July 14, 1799,   Richard Sanders and Mary Anne Smither
August 30, 1799,   Richard B. Johnson and Lucetta Massey
November 25, 1799,   John Brinnon and Elizabeth Crenshaw
August 12, 1799, Mordica Hallbrooker and Sarah Marmaduke,
    Sam'l Templeman, her guardian, gives his consent
October 8, 1800, William Robinson and Nancy Washington, John
    Rose, his guardian, gives his consent
March 3, 1801,   John McKey and Margaret Spence
March 2, 1801,   William Deatley and Ellen Briscoe
April 28, 1800, Reuben Beale and Eliza Taylor Turberville, Thos.
    Chilton, her guardian, gives his consent
October 17, 1800,   Henry Jackson and Harriot Stuart
September 22, 1800,   Charles Sanford and Sabina Rose
September 26, 1800,   Reuben Potter and Ellon Briscoe
April 23, 1800,   Frederick Alverson and Caty Doulman
April 13, 1800,   James S. Cook and Sarah Edmonds
September 20, 1800,   John Beddoo and Nancy Bolderson
December 11, 1800, Vincent Barrick and Elizabeth Weeks, Benja-
    min Pope Weeks, her father, gives his consent
December 2, 1800,   William Watson and Catty Collins
March 13, 1800,   Gerrard Hopkins and Elizabeth S. Theids
May 9, 1800,   John Kew and Mary Pursley
July 26, 1800,   Robert Bennett and Jane Lefevre
October, 27, 1800,   Peter Gallagher and Betsy Garner
December 28, 1800,   John Jones and Nancy Burruss
January 19, 1800,   John S. Tapscott and Elizabeth Attwell
December 10, 1801,   Daniel Morriss and Betsey Sutton
March 23, 1801,   James Johnson and Elizabeth Morriss
December 23, 1801, Samuel Hunter and Nancy Muse, Ann Muse,
    her mother, gives her consent
April 27, 1801, George Curtis and Nancy Doleman, Lidea Dole-
    man, her mother, gives her consent
March 21, 1801,   John Brown and Elizabeth Brown
October 15, 1801,   James Ryals and Elizabeth Brinnon
April 9, 1801,   Richard Steel and Susanna Monroe
March 17, 1801,   Jarrard McKey and Winny Davis

March 21, 1801,	Youel Howson and Alesy Howel
November 16, 1801,	George Nash and Sally Mitchell
November 10, 1801,	James Pursley and Sarah Green
September 28, 1801,	Robert Hudson and Martha King
November, 1801,	John Barrot and Elizabeth Mullins
October 25, 1801,	William S. Neale and Nancy Neale
November 6, 1801,	George Sutton and Nancy Packett
————————1801,	Jesse Pursley and Winney Yardley
August 19, 1801,	John Mothershead and Celia Massey
July 17, 1801,	William Luttrell and Keziah Marmaduke
July 27, 1801,	John McGinnis and Sally Hedley
June 22, 1801,	William Northon and Lucy Yeatman
December 31, 1800,	Birdett Eskridge and Anne Washington

October 12, 1801, John Graham and Molly Middleton, Peter P.
Cox, her guardian, gives his consent

December 24, 1801, Wm. Marmaduke and Polly Dafane, Vincent
Dafane, her father, gives his consent

December 22, 1801,	Smith King and Anne Lamkin
December 9, 1801,	George Cooper and Sarah Wells
————————1801,	John Danks and Nancy Pilbert
January 4, 1802,	Cupid Jordan and Lucy Adams
August 26, 1801,	Fielding Owens and Polly Weeks
June 22, 1801,	Vincent Daffron and Sarah Doleman
January 16, 1800,	Richard Neale and Mary Smith
December 22, 1800,	James Figget and Hannah McKenny
July 17, 1801,	Andrew Montgomery and Nancy Hall
December 25, 1801,	Thomas Stowers and Sarah Butler
January 6, 1801,	William Spark and Lucy Redman

January 5, 1801, James Otlay and Margaret Dickie, John Dickie,
her father, gives his consent

December 13, 1801, George Moore and Hannah Smith, John
Smith, her father, gives his consent

August 24, 1801, Pope Tiffey and Elizabeth Vegar

————————1801, Presley Hinson and Caty Peed, Phillip Peed, her
father, gives his consent

March 3, 1801, Lamkin Lacy and Elizabeth Morse

November 17, 1800, John Pursley and Sarah Washington, Wm.
Washington and Elizabeth Washington, her parents, give
their consent

June 25, 1801, Samuel Wroe and Molley King, Wm. King, her
father, gives his consent

June 2, 1801, Isaac Johnston and Betsey Hinson, Joshua Hinson,
    her father, gives his consent
August 27, 1801, Benjamin Courtney and Mary Smith, Jeremiah
    Smith, her father, gives his consent
June 2, 1801,   Thomas Newman and Peggy Bartlett
October 3, 1801, Spencer Fegget and Mary Dodd, Joseph Dodd,
    her father, gives his consent
October 20, 1801,   Herman Jenkins and Cathrine Carter
September 19, 1801, William Brann and Keziah Jewell, Eliza
    Jewell, her mother, gives her consent
October 13, 1801,   Reuben Spurling and Molly Pumroy
April 15, 1801, Robert Sanford and Sally Clarke, Jemimah Clarke,
    her mother, gives her consent
October 10, 1802, Thomas G. Watkins and Susan Jackson, Saml
    Jackson, her father, gives his consent
October 18, 1802,   James Brewer and Nansy Richardson
May 17, 1802, John B. Fulk and Nancy Mozingo, Sarah Mozingo,
    her mother, gives her consent
December 21, 1801, James Stephens and Nancy Douglas, John
    Douglas, her father, gives his consent
June 16, 1802,   Peter P. Cox and Sally Gordon
July 10, 1802,   Wm. Enniss and Margret Brinn
February 10, 1802,   Joel S. Rose and Franky Rice
March 8, 1802,   William Willson and Elizabeth Hinson
December 28, 1801, John Norwood and Sally Brickey, William
    Brickey, her father, gives his consent
January 25, 1802,   William T. Sanders and Frances Weaver
July 27, 1802,   Richard Stuart and Margaret McCarty
February 2, 1802, Nelson Cridlen and Nancy White, William
    White, her father, gives his consent
July 7, 1802,   William Sanford and Elender Dolman
December 12, 1803,   Leven Jones and Frances Hall
July 13, 1803,   Danl. Sanford and Rutha McGinniss
July 7, 1803,   John S. Tapscott and Sally Cain
————1803,   Martin Tapscott and Elizabeth Cox
September 12, 1803,   Rodham Hall and Magdalen McClanaham
—————, 1803,   Peter Rust Lamkin and Elizabeth King
March 13, 1802,   William Robinson and Sally McKenney
January 15, 1803, Henry L. Jacobs and Peggy Garner, Samuel
    Garner, her father, gives his consent
————————1803,   Claiburne Baber and Hannah C. Crabb

June 27, 1803,   Jesse Marth and Polly Jackson, Elizabeth Jackson, her mother, gives her consent

January 28, 1803,   Meredith M. Hackney and Elizabeth T. Rust, Elizabeth Rust, her mother, gives her consent

————————,   Thos. Bowing and Molly Hinson

————————,   John Silby and Sally Fones

August 23, 1803,   Hugh Quinlen and Judith B. Thompson

January 25, 1803,   Beverly Robinson and Sally Cox

January 26, 1803,   Vincent Marmaduke and Betsy B. Blundell, Thomas Blundell, her father, gives his consent

July 18, 1803,   George Christopher and Ann Beale

December 10, 1803,   William Standley and Frances Walker

February 6, 1804,   John Alton and Lucinde Butler, Lucynda Butler, her mother, gives her consent

June 25,1803,   Jennings Hinson and Fanny Weadon, Thomas Weadon, her father, gives his consent

November 22, 1803,   Vincent Reynolds and Hadassah Hazzard, Wm. Hazzard, her father, gives his consent

February 13, 1804,   John M. Smith and Meriah Thompson

July 16, 1803,   William Butler and Amey Weston

November 26, 1803,   George W. Tenant and Ann Campbell, Susanna Campbell, her mother, gives her consent

September 18, 1803,   William Sanders and Anne Playl

March 6, 1803,   Daniel Saunders and Mary Bragg

————1803,   Reuben Hart and Elizabeth Thomas

December 19, 1803,   Reuben Briscoe and Ann B. Johnston, Samuel Johnston, her father, gives his consent

October 20, 1803,   Daniel Barker and Lucy Smith, Ann Smith, her mother, gives her consent

October 26, 1803,   William McKildoe and Polly Self

September 26, 1803,   Doctor George Fitzhugh and Lucy Stuart

October 14, 1802,   Brooks Mothershead and Matilda Fegget

March 12, 1803,   Spencer Mullins and Mary Brawner

November 25, 1802,   James Wilson and Sally Hughsencraft

March 22, 1803,   Josiah Hazard and Fanny Lewis Ramey

————1803,   Linsey Courtney and Caty Garner

December 20, 1803,   Willis Garner and Magdalene Crabb

December 28, 1803,   John Mitchell and Roseanny Carpenter, John Carpenter, her father, gives his consent

November 15, 1803,   Benjamin Askins and Jane Grant

November 7, 1803,   James Montgomery and Elizabeth Hall

April 10, 1803,   John Goode and Sally Betterworth
March 28, 1803,   Bennett Rose and Nancy Brickey, Wm. Brickey,
    her father, gives his consent
April 20, 1804,   Zachariah Pritchett and Peggy Clutten, William
    Clutten, her father, gives his consent
September 4, 1804,   Reuben Reynolds and Elizabeth Thomas
December 30, 1804,   Starks Moore and Fanny Annandale
September 1, 1804,   Samuel Fryer and Haney Ennis
May 5, 1804,   Edward Willson and Lucy Fones
September 1, 1804,   William Howsen and Betsy McKenney
January 3, 1804,   John Barrot and Martha Sanford
August 22, 1804,   James Tate and Charity Grimes
March 14, 1804,   Caleb Rice and Sabinah Rigg
September 21, 1805,   George Smith and Betsy Batton, James Bat-
    ten, her father gives his consent
June 11, 1804,   William Olive and Rebecca Muse
August 9, 1804,   Henry Deatley and Sally Tate
May 15, 1804,   Thomas Pope Basye and Hannah Lee Turberville,
    Martha Turberville, her mother, gives her consent
May 8, 1804   John Gutridge and Elizabeth Crask
June 12, 1804,   James Cox and Hannah Jackson
————1804,   Jeremiah Jeffrice and Jane Jeffrice
December 28, 1804,   James T. Brown and Polly Sandy
October 15, 1804,   William Colliston and Kissey Johnson
July 30, 1804,   William Hall and Molly Olive
June 5, 1804,   Richard Potts and Martha Willson, Henry Willson,
    her father, gives his consent
June 13, 1804,   William Bunyan and Nancy Bell Self, Job Self, her
    father, gives his consent
December 31, 1804,   John B. Jenkins and Winifred L. Payne
February 16, 1804,   Benjamin Porter and Polly Templeman
March 7, 1804,   Andrew Pullin and Rebecca Wilson
September 29, 1804,   Lewis Briant and Jane Caddeen
December 10, 1804,   James Wigley and Elizabeth Barrott
December 21, 1804,   James Sutton and Molley Hawkins
January 17, 1805,   Jonathan Hawkins and Elender Sullivan
June 18, 1805,   William Annandale and Elizabeth Dodd
————1805,   William Tate and ——— Pumroy
December 17, 1805,   Presley Garner and Caty Askins
————1806,   Wm. Ryals and Elizabeth Carter
April 4, 1805,   James Donehaw and Elender Fones

December 24, 1805,   George Deatley and Lucinda Alton

August 6, 1805,   George Courtney and Hannah Rice

September 5, 1805,   Newman McKenny and Alice McGuire

February 12, 1805,   James S. Mothershead and Sally Riley

January 14, 1805,   William Williams and Margaret Branson, Newyear Branson, her father, gives his consent

October 28, 1805,   George B. Danks and Priscilla Pritchett

December 20, 1805,   Thomas Neale and Patsey Hart

February 17, 1805,   Ebenezer Selby and Nancy Brown

March 20, 1805,   Samuel Garner and Sarah Billings

January 28, 1805,   William Franklin and Nancy White

February 5, 1805,   James Dozier and Betsey Muse, Thom. Muse, her father, gives his consent

October 9, 1805,   John Burgess and Nancy Benson

November 29, 1805,   George Boon and Mary Berkley

February 13, 1805,   Jeremiah Edmond and Molly Harris

October 9, 1805,   Harrison Burgess and Frances Wood

December 23, 1805,   Thos. Williams and Jane Garner

November 25, 1805,   Willis Garner and Frances G. Lamkin

December 3, 1805,   William Brinham and Caty Moreton

November 16, 1805,   Richard Bram and Jane Curk

June 10, 1805,   William Spence and Winny Sisson

April 24, 1805,   Robert Anderson and Treasy Carrell

July 10, 1805,   John Jewett and Barbary McKenney

October 28, 1805,   John Payne and Elizabeth Washington

July 10, 1805,   Rodham Neale and Rose Smith, John Strother, her guardian, gives his consent

October 31, 1805,   Joseph Read and Polly Wigley

October 28, 1805,   George McKye and Hannah B. Aston

June 8, 1805,   John H. Doleman and Frances Bayne Vigar

February 25, 1805,   James Jett and Nancy Muse, Thomas Muse, her father, gives his consent

January 23, 1805,   Barney Beckwith and Elizabeth P. Martin

April 30, 1806,   John Billings and Mary Self

September 14, 1806,   James Simms and Nancy Johnson, Elizabeth Johnson, her mother, gives her consent

August 25, 1806,   Richard Wilkins and Susannah Deatley

August 15, 1806,   George C. Sedwick and Sally Hall

July 21, 1806,   William Marks and Betsy Jenkins

January 6, 1806,   Henry Marston and Sally Carrell

January 28, 1806,   Daniel Garner and Nancy Brann

April 14, 1806, William Asbury and Mary Muse, Thom. Muse, her father, gives his consent

January 28, 1806, John Cowart and Elizabeth Redman

May 19, 1806, Thomas Morgan and Leannah Burgess

February 18, 1806, John Scoonover and Fanny Drake

October 3, 1806, John Mullins and Anna M. Weaver, Rachel Weaver, her mother, gives her consent

October 20, 1806, Daniel Willson and Rebecca Bartlett

November 18, 1806, Reuben Olive and Polly Head, Isaac Head and Rachel Head, her parents, give their consent

December 9, 1806, Spencer B. Worth and Nancy Curtis

December 2, 1806, Vincent McGuire and Frances McKenny

November 5, 1806, Charles Barn and Hannah Neale, Mary Neale, her mother, gives her consent

April 26, 1806, Thomas Mathany and Mary W. Courtney

June 11, 1806, Thos. Weaver and Mary Anidale

January 25, 1806, John Missick and Susan Kirck, John Lyell, her guardian, gives his consent

May 15, 1806, Barnet Good and Elizabeth Weaver, Thos. Weaver, her father, gives his consent

April 27, 1806, John Weaver and Sabrey Bryant

January 12, 1806, Edmund Walker and Elizabeth S. Packett, John Lyell, her guardian, gives his consent

March 3, 1806, William Jett and Pheby Short, Jeremiah Short and Paty Short, her parents, give their consent

May 6, 1806, George Rust and Ursla P. Robinson

April 21, 1806, Christopher J. Collins and Elizabeth Washington Lendrum, Thomas Lendrum, her father, gives his consent

September 16, 1806, Abraham Silvey and Elizabeth Spilmon, Betsy Spilmon, her mother, gives her consent

December 16, 1806, Samuel Davis and Fanny Smith

May 12, 1805, Stephen Jett and Elizabeth D. Muse, Thomas Muse, her father, gives her consent

December 30, 1806, Alexander Nash and Penelope Bartlett, Joseph Bartlett, her father, gives his consent

October 2, 1806, Robinson McGuire and Mary Hall, John Hall and Sarah Hall, her parents, give their consent

December 15, 1806, Vincent Reynolds and Frances Sisson

December 12, 1806, Edmond Tate and Peggy Asston

December 21, 1806, William Carpenter and Mary Cavender

September 20, 1806, Francis Self and Ann Thrift

December 24, 1806,   James Newman and Jane Knott

December 16, 1806,   James McKenny and Sally Sutton

March 27, 1806,   Richard T. Brown and Lucy Spark

November 13, 1806,   Thos. Croxton and Eliza B. Spence

April 1, 1806,   William B. Smith and Nancy Butlor, John Smith, her guardian, gives his consent

December 8, 1807,   Saml. Lyell and Peggy S. McKildoe

December 24, 1807,   George A. W. Johnston and Ann F. Johnson

November 25, 1807,   William Jett and Catharine White, Susanna White, her mother, gives her consent

December 5, 1807,   John Davis and Elizabeth Lacy, Thomas Lacy, her father, gives his consent

December 18, 1807,   Burnett Thompson and Barbara Bell

————1807,   Saml. Coats and Lucy Gaunder

October 15, 1807,   Stephen Brann and Peggy Hawkins

March 14, 1807,   Charles Scott and Rebecca McClanahan

December 21, 1807,   Enock Finch and Elizabeth Muse Moxley

January 1, 1807,   Joseph Selby and Nancy Ambrose, Eligah Ambrose, her father, gives his consent

March 3, 1807,   George Hail and Fanny Cavender

December 23, 1807,   Benedict Wright and Hannah Claughton

August 18, 1807,   Thomas A. Sorrell and Nancy Attwell, William Attwell, her father, gives his consent

November 23, 1804,   Wm. C. Chandler and Sally R. Crabbe

December 17, 1807,   Gennings Yeatman and Nancy Bashaw

September 9, 1807,   Daniel Carter and Nomey Fones

February 12, 1807,   Daniel Moxley and Fanny Branham

August 8, 1808,   Henry L. Yeatman and Alice Monroe, David Monroe, her father, gives his consent

October 7, 1807,   Bartlett Scates and Susanna Bartlett

March 3, 1807,   Christopher Collins and Fanny Pierce

August 4, 1807,   Samuel Templeman and Caty McKenney

March 16, 1807,   Edward Sutton and Sally Anthony

April 3, 1809,   John A Smith and Lettia Lee, Thomas Jones, her guardian, gives his consent

September 22, 1807,   Walter Waughan and Polly McKy, James McKy and Mary McKy, her parents, give their consent

November 3, 1807,   Cornelius Beazley and Jane R. Rust

December 19, 1807,   Bennett Rose and Agness Barber

October 10, 1807,   John M. McNeil and Lucy Moxley, C. Moxley, her father, gives his consent

December 15, 1807, Alexander Garner and Lettie Garner
December 23, 1807, William Mitchell and Susannah Muse, James
Muse, her father, gives his consent
June 9, 1806, William Berkley and Susannah Muse
February 10, 1807, Gerard McKenney and Peggy Sisson
February 5, 1807, Elliott Porter and Frances Edwards, Frankey
Edwards, her mother, gives her consent
May 16, 1807, James Hinson and Sibella Washington, William
Washington and Betsy Washington, her parents, give their
consent
December 13, 1807, Thomas Pegg and Harriott Bruce
July 22, 1807, William M. Walker and Sibella P. Fields
April 7, 1807, Joseph Lacy and Patsy Hammock Scott, Charles
Scott, her father, gives his consent
—————1807, John Sanders and Nancy France, John France,
and Caty France, her parents, give their consent
January 10, 1807, Thos. Gregory and Elizabeth Cavender
December 22, 1807, Charles Mothershead and Keziah Pendergrass
June 17, 1807, George Foorde and Nancy Poosy
February 10, 1807, William Johnston and Ann Deane
December 19, 1807, Thomas Sanders and Bartlett Fones
————— —, 1807, John Balderson and Caty Edmond
June 22, 1807, James Thomas and Darky Thomas
July 20, 1807, Robert Sanford and Susannah Fox
November 4, 1807, William Coats and Franky Carpenter
September 16, 1807, James H. Bailey and Harriott McNeil
February 10, 1807, Charles Fones and Elinor Muse
December 29, 1807, Bolling Fitzhugh and Fanny Fitzhugh, George
Fitzhugh, her father, gives his consent
December 8, 1807, Thomas Brown and Fanny Brown
October 6, 1808, William Habron and Sally Pillien
July 4, 1808, William Lawrence and Ursley Sanford
February 1, 1808, Reuben Bruce and Martha Bayne
May 12, 1808, Jeremiah Rochester and Molly F. Northern
January 6, 1808, William Hall and Betsy Shadrack, Elizabeth
Shadrack, her mother, gives her consent
January 4, 1808, George McCoy and Nancy McCoy, Bennett Mc-
Coy, her father, gives his consent
March 7, 1808, James Carpenter and Susanna Beland
February 22, 1808, Eligah Scates and ——— Newman
January 13, 1808, Thomas Dozier and Frances Jones

March 28, 1808,   Thomas Jenkins and Sarah Green
January —, 1808,   James Saunders and ——— Carpenter
April 4, 1808,   William Hall and Caty Bruce
September 26, 1808,   Richard Battin and Eliza Edwards
January 13, 1808,   Trusel Hall and Hannah Middleton
January 16, 1808, Thomas Omohundro and Nancy B. Blundell, Thomas Blundell, her father, gives his consent
July 14, 1808,   James C. Anthony and Mary Lee
August 17, 1808,   Peter P. Cox and Eleanor Jackson
December 25, 1809,   Berryman Balderson and Elizabeth Fones
April 19, 1808,   Saml. Mothershead and Margaret Kendall
October 31, 1808,   John Jenkins and Rebecca Brown, Hannah Brown, her mother, gives her consent
October 24, 1808,   Jesse Monroe and Peggy Thously
February 16, 1808,   William Bunolp and Jane Smith, Mary Nelson, her guardian, gives her consent
July 13, 1808, Edward Ensco and Elizabeth Burgess, Dan'l Burgess, her father, gives his consent
December 29, 1808, William True and Elizabeth Weldon, George Weldon, her father, gives his consent
May 7, 1808,   James Jewell and Nancy Brewer
May 24, 1808,   Peter Gordon and Susan Lee
March 1, 1808,   Robt. G. Robb and Eve Bankhead
December 23, 1808,   James Miller and Peggy Hipkins
December 22, 1808,   James Weaver and Ailsey Sutton
June 27, 1808,   John Hollinshead and Elinor Steel
December 7, 1808, John Campbell and Eliza Ferguson Murphy, John Murphy, her father, gives his consent
July 13, 1808, Charles Scott and Fanny Newman, James B. Newman, her father, gives his consent
January 13, 1808,   Thomas Moss and Nancy Eidson
May 16, 1808,   Thomas Cavender and Sarah Scinnor
January 27, 1808,   James Bartlett and Sarah Troop
September 14, 1808, Esau Pomroy and Elizabeth Green, Charles Green, her father, gives his consent
December 12, 1808,   Marks Crask and Mary Payne
December 23, 1808, John Crask and Shady Carpenter, John Carpenter, her father, gives his consent
May 27, 1808,   James Johnston and Elizabeth Davis
December 8, 1808,   James Deane and Leanner Washington
May 20, 1808,   Dan'l Marmaduke and Nancy T. Dishman

February 8, 1809, William Harper and Polly Self, Molley Self, her
    mother, gives her consent

February 10, 1809, John H. Yeatman and Mary Burgess

November 30, 1809, Sherrod James and Fanny Deatley, James
    Deatley, her father, gives his consent

December 27, 1809, Thomas Franklin and Nancy Hale

April 10, 1809, James Mothershead and Jane Spilman, Margaret
    Mothershead, his mother, gives her consent

August 15, 1809, James Peed and Caty Drake

June 22, 1809, Robert B. Courtney and Nancy Carvin

————1809, Thos. Spence and Mary C. Brown

December 25, 1809, John Johnson and Hany Tate

December 24, 1810, William Pearch and Nancy Thompson

December 14, 1809, Dabney Baber and Jane Crabb

May 26, 1809, George Ashton and Elizabeth Jett, Wm. Storke
    Jett, father, gives his consent

December 19, 1809, Wm. M. Crabb and Sally Lee Randolph

December 11, 1809, Edward Spence and Sally Sissin

December 1, 1809, Wm. Jewell and Mary Carroll

March 5, 1810 Joseph Dodd and Elizabeth Bryant

July 30, 1810, John Hinson and Polly Kelly, Molley Kelly, her
    mother, gives her consent

July 8, 1810, Rodham Moxley and Mary Weldon

March 1, 1810, William White and Ann Dishman, William Dish-
    man, her father, gives his consent

March 21, 1810, John Steward and Fanny Hore

March 26, 1810, John Barker and ———— Gutridge

June 11, 1810, Edward Wright and Sally Silby

March 1, 1810, William Dishman and Elizabeth White

March 5, 1810, Frederick Alverson and Nancy Carroll

October 4, 1810, William King and Ann King

July 9, 1810, Allen S. Dozier and Nancy Shackleford

December 20, 1810, Thomas Oharro and Nancy Bunyan

February 9, 1810, Francis C. Triplett and Sarah Mariner

January 25, 1810, Jeremiah Thrift and Elizabeth Self, William
    Self and Frances Self, her parents, give their consent

May 11, 1810, Thos. Whittington and Frances Nelms Turner,
    Snsanna Hall, her mother, gives her consent

January 10, 1810, Jesse Muse and Rebecca Brown

September 11, 1810, John Bailey and Nancy Mathany

February 20, 1810, Alexander F. Rose and Mildred W. Rose

January 15, 1810,   Samuel Brann and Polly Thomas, Susann Thomas, her mother, gives her consent

December 19, 1809,   Daniel Jenkins and Sarah Silvey

December 21, 1809,   Thomas Brown and Eliza Simpson

October 19, 1809, George Coats and Peggy McKenny, Danl. McKenny and Mary McKenny, her parents, give their consent

January 7, 1809,   Alexander Weaver and Harriott Anandale

October 18, 1809,   William Moore and Hannah Beale

July 9, 1810,   William Piper and Elizabeth Jett Brown

December 17, 1810,   William Yardly and Nancy Pumroy

December 14, 1810,   James Berkley and Hannah Brinnon

December 4, 1810,   Joseph Barker and Elizabeth Hall, William Hall and Anna Hall, her parents, give their consent

October 28, 1809,   Jeremiah Sanford and Harriot Weaver

February 26, 1810,   Robert Jenkins and Hannah Muse

June 6, 1810,   Charles Callahan and Alice Hyland

November 27, 1810,   James M. Clerky and Elizabeth S. Moxley

January 1, 1809,   Benedict Walker and Charlotte Smith

January 15, 1810,   James H. Jenkins and Peggy Gutridge, Thomas Gutridge, her father, gives his consent

May 27, 1810,   Spencer Lucas and Jane Yardley

January 1, 1810,   Marks Crank and Caty Collins

March 24, 1810,   Jesse Bowing and Nancy Kelley, Molly Kelley, her mother, gives her consent

November 19, 1810,   John W. Hungerford and Sophia Muse, Walk. Muse, her father, gives his consent

December 23, 1809,   James Abbott and Fanny Jeffries

January 7, 1809,   Wm. Mothershead and Alice Mothershead, George Mothershead and Sary Mothershead, her parents, give their consent

February 4, 1809,   James Johnson and Mary Turner Branson

November 27, 1809, George Quesenbury and Jane Carter Pope, Lawr. Pope, her father, gives his consent

January 26, 1809,   Reuben Sanford and Judah Sanders, Patty Sanders, her mother, gives her consent

December 30, 1809,   Saml. Tate and Harwar Lucas

March 6, 1810,   John Gregory and Elizabeth Carrel

January 9, 1809,   Charles Rice and Elender Ford Smith, John Smith, her father, gives his consent

December 14, 1809,   William Jett and Nancy Thomas

February 4, 1809,   William Butler and Polly Stoot

February 3, 1809, Travis McGuire and Becky Sutton

July 5, 1809, James Antony and Rebecca Billins, Robert Antony, his father, gives his consent

June 9, 1809, Barrett Sisson and Frances Brown

May 8, 1809, John Maxwell and Olivia Ann Mitchell, William Forbes, her guardian, gives his consent

February 3, 1809, John McGuire and Mary Pillsbury, Sally Pillsbury, her mother, gives her consent

September 22, 1809, Thos. Jackson and Polly Brown

January 16, 1810, John Arnest and Anne Martin Maund, H. L. Maund, her father, gives his consent

December 2, 1810, Foxhall Sturman and Elizabeth Neale, Ann Neale, her mother, gives her consent

October 11, 1810, Newyear Branson and Fanny Brinnon

January 23, 1809, Thomas Doleman and Sally Hazzard

February 2, 1811, Geo. Gregory and Molly Billings

November 6, 1811, Thomas Barber and Lucy Mothershead, Isabella Mothershead, her mother, gives her consent

December 23, 1811, Peter N. Rust and Polly Morse

December 31, 1811, James Anthony and Elizabeth Goode

February 4, 1811, Wm. Anderson and Peggy Fisher

December 31, 1811, George Bevelton and Penny Lucas

March 19, 1811, James R. Nash and Martha Caddeen

April 23, 1811, Thos. Olliff and Elizabeth Curtis

May 17, 1811, David Wardrobe and Polly Mezick

January 9, 1811, Jeremiah Short and Nelley Hollinshead

February 14, 1811, Alexander McGuire and Elizabeth Sutton

September 16, 1811, Joseph Dozier and Sally Muse

January 24, 1811, Thomas Inscoe and Frances Bailey

October 1811, Saml. C. Anandale and Cynthia Branson, Newyear Branson, her father, gives his consent

December 29, 1811, Jonathan Bowen and Sarah Paris

January 20, 1811, Wm. Self and Polly Kent

November 7, 1811, Meredith Payne and Sarah Steward

August 22, 1811, Dozier Lyell and Fanny Smith, Peggy Smith, her mother, gives her consent

January 11, 1811, Peter Colloson and Susan Simms

January 2, 1811, William Barrett and Jane Smith

December 21, 1811, Henry Brawner and Ann Caddeen

January 8, 1811, Bennett Rose and Sally S. Self, Wm. Self, her father, gives his consent

January 7, 1811,   Steptoe Pickett and Sarah O. Chilton, Geo.
    Christopher, her guardian, gives his consent
March 28, 1811,   John Collingsworth and Fanny Collingsworth
January 1, 1811,   Matthew Yeatman and Eleanor Gaune
March 5, 1811,   Joseph Sutton and Martha Crask
June 4, 1811,   Charles Hazzard and Ann Rice Rigmaden
August 30, 1811,   Elijah Sanford and Peggy Sanford
November 27, 1811,   Charles Mothershead and Winnifred Jenkins
January 23, 1812,   William Nash and Caty Hinson, James Hinson
    and Nancy Hinson, her parents, give their consent
March 23, 1812,   George Butler and Nelly Laycock
March 10, 1812,   John Barrett and Elizabeth Briscoe
March 4, 1812,   James Gregory and Isabella Templeman
February 27, 1812,   George Walker and Sally Robinson, Joseph
    Robinson, her father, gives his consent
September 15, 1812,   Daniel Sanford and Mary Weaver
April 15, 1812,   Thomas J. Bulger and Nancy Hall
July 28, 1812,   Thomas Wheatley and Alcy Collinsworth, Wm.
    Collinsworth, her father, gives his consent
December 27, 1812,   James Robinson and Sally A. Crenshaw, Da-
    vid Crenshaw, her father, gives his consent
December 16, 1812,   Wm. Askings and Sally Beale, Saml Beale,
    her father, gives his consent
October 4, 1812,   William Marks and Nancy Wingfield
September 18, 1812,   John Redman and Alice Deatley
September 28, 1812,   John Ridles and Sally Head, Isaac Head and
    Rachel Head, her parents, give their consent
May 16, 1812,   Coleman Pitts and Nancy Dickerson
———————1812,   Tarply Nash and Elizabeth Burgess
November 4, 1812,   Reuben Sanford and Mary Willson
September 7, 1812,   Elijah Knox and Frances Alverson, Zacha-
    riah Alverson and Kissiah Alverson, her parents, give their
    consent
September 7, 1812,   James Nash and Elizabeth Hill; John Hill and
    Elender Hill, her parents, give their consent
December 7, 1812,   Wm. Olliff and Eleanor Pulin
January 31, 1812,   Charles Taliaferro and Susannah Moxley, Ann
    Moxley, her mother, gives her consent
April 22, 1812,   Alexander Berryman and Catherine Berryman;
    Thos. N. Berryman, his father and her guardian, gives his
    consent

January 25, 1812,   James Gutridge and Nancy Spilman
March 20, 1812,   Samuel Newman and Jenny Johnson
December 29, 1812,   George Newman and Lucy Youn Buckley
April 25, 1812, Richard Wright and Polly Attwell, William Attwell, her father, gives his consent
March 29, 1813, Thos. D. Covington and Mary R. Stowers, Thomas Stowers, her father, gives his consent
November 24, 1813,   Wesley Butler and Frances T. Crask
April 26, 1813, Benjamin White and Mary Quesenbury, Wm. Quesenbury, her father, gives his consent
November 30, 1813,   Fred'k Newman and Scilla Carey
August 4, 1813, Jesse Kendall and Sukey Sanford, Joshua Sanford, her father, gives his consent
December 11, 1813,   John Crenshaw and Betsy Norwood
March 5, 1813,   Robt. Jinkins and Betsy B. Mitchell
August 9, 1813, Thos. Scutt and Molley Howell, Thomas Gregory, her guardian, gives his consent
June 22, 1813, Ludwell Nash and Sally Barnett, Geo. Glascock, her guardian, gives his consent
December 21, 1813,   William Johnson and Molley Redman
August 10, 1813,   Thomas Jenkins and Mary Hill
February 25, 1813,   Nathaniel King and Elizabeth Briscoe
June 14, 1813,   Newman Hammons and Nancy Green
August 7, 1813, John Hunter and Susan Edwards, Frances Edwards, her mother, gives her consent
November 3, 1813, John Norwood and Sally Porter, Edward Porter, her father, gives his consent
————1813, James Coats and Elizabeth Carpenter, John Carpenter, her father, gives his consent
January 25, 1812,   Washington G. Mariner and Leanna Kew
July 26, 1813,   William Wheatley and Sally Brinnon
July 29, 1813,   Peter Davis and Elizabeth Shirley
June 1, 1813, John Brinnon and Elizabeth Steel, Jno. B. Steel, her father, gives his consent
December 21, 1813,   Richard N. Mariner and Ann Bispham
December 21, 1813,   John T. Brown and Elizabeth Hennage
March 8, 1813, Fineas Lefever and Abby Peed, Alesay Peed, her mother, gives her consent
July 5, 1813,   Beckham Thomas and Nelly Anthony
August 12, 1813,   Armstrong McKenny and Jane Steward
January 27, 1813,   Jno. Underwood and Francis Washington

March 22, 1813,   William Courtney and Nancy Crenshaw

March 29, 1813,   John Harrison and Judith Leycock, Samuel Harrison, his father, gives his consent

February 14, 1814,   Vincent Douglas and Hannah King, Wm. King, her father, gives his consent

January 26, 1814,   Harry Greggs and Barbara Lucas

February 28, 1814,   Robert Long and Polly Hazzard

April 25, 1814,   George V. Hudson and Lettice Carter

February 9, 1814,   Thomas Franklin and Harriet Sutton

May 23, 1814,   Richard Clark and Sally B. Smith, Peter Smith, her father, gives his consent

May 25, 1814,   Robert Middleton and Louisa H. Hall

May 30, 1814,   Vincent Jones and Martha Jenkins

July 11, 1814,   Thomas S. Davis and Eliza Davis, Elizabeth Davis, her mother, gives her consent

November 28, 1814,   John Bayne and Ellen Tiffey

January 24, 1814,   Blain Aston and Priscy Weldon

November 28, 1814,   John Blackwell and Frances Parker

October 7, 1814,   Joshua Sanford and Lucy Wilson

October 24, 1814,   Richard Wilkins and Jane Mitchell

June 16, 1814,   Thornton Connally and Betsy S. Acred

June 16, 1814,   George G. Mothershead and Catharine Crask

————1814,   James Yardley and Elizabeth Edmonds, James Edmonds, her father, gives his consent

June 22, 1814,   Joshua Reamy and Meriah Neale, John Neale, her father, gives his consent

June 23, 1814,   James Alderson and Jane Baber

July 13, 1814,   William Nelson and Ann E. Douglas

May 26, 1814,   Thomas Fouke and Susanna Baker

December 26, 1814,   Owen Brinnon and Elizabeth Palmer

December 27, 1814,   Allen Sanders and Martha F. Newman

September 28, 1814,   John Brinn and Peggy Coale

January 23, 1815,   Elisha Spurling and Elizabeth M. Cary

December 31, 1814,   William Barrott and Felicia Pegg

December 9, 1814,   Clark Short and Nancy Alverson

January 15, 1814,   William Butler and Margaret Jacobs

December 16, 1814,   Sam'l Mothershead and Eliza T. Richardson

January 15, 1814,   John Potter and Elizabeth Newman

October 5, 1814,   James Winkfield and Winney Hammons

December 23, 1815,   Meredith Carpenter and Jane Saunders

December 19, 1815, Reuben Hall and Winney Knash, Nancy Knash, her mother, gives her consent

December 20, 1815, Spencer Miller and Nancy S. Moxley, John R. McNeil, her guardian, gives her consent

September 20, 1815, George Hinson and Elizabeth Tate

October 4, 1815, George Daniel and Magdalen

October 11, 1815, Daniel Foxall and Sibbener Lawrence

October 18, 1815, George Henry and Ellen Jackson

October 14, 1815, Stephen Read and Nancy S. Dozier

November 8, 1815, Joseph Dodd and Elizabeth Mothershead

October 26, 1815, Samuel R. Fones and Nancy Wilson

November 15, 1815, Jacob Miller and Lucinda Neale

November 15, 1815, Daniel Payne and Sarah Cox, Peter P. Cox, her guardian, gives his consent

November 27, 1815, William Headley and Louisa Middleton

September 28, 1815, Thomas Sandy and Isabella Beale

January 4, 1815, Thomas Bartlett and Polly Mothershead, John Mothershead, her father, gives his consent

February 7, 1815, George Mothershead and Polly Howe, Ann Howe, her mother, gives her consent

December 28, 1815, Newman B. Jackson and Mary Garner

December 28, 1815, Amme Kelton and Nancy Fisher

April 12, 1815, James Pratt and Alcy Oliff

August 18, 1815, George Watson and Hannah Brawner

June 8, 1815, Presley Cox and Sally Ricarda Lee

August 21, 1815, Le Roy P. Daingerfield and Juliet O. Parker, Wm. H. Parker, her father, gives his consent

August 15, 1815, Joseph G. Jewett and Nancy Strother

August 3, 1814, Henry Gregory and Nancy Barnett

June 7, 1815, Richard Bulger and Polly Jackson

June 1, 1815, James Hinson and Susannah Sanford

July 31, 1815, James Yardley and Joyce Lucas

August 12, 1815, William Deatley and Lucinda Deatley, Christopher Deatley, her father, gives his consent

July 26, 1815, George Johnson and Milley V, Dye,

September 30, 1815, John B. Pope and Cynthia Annandale

December 27, 1815, Joseph Coates and Nancy Sanford

May 22, 1815, William Sanders and Suky Marks, James Marks and Frances Marks, her parents, give their consent

May 3, 1815, John Spilman and Thirsa Holt, Richard N. Mariner, her guardian, gives his consent

March 4, 1815,   John S. Carter and Eliza Ann Harrison
May 5, 1815,   James Mariner and Lucy Weldon
May 22, 1815,   William Burgess and Nancy Bragg
May 30, 1815,   William Willson and Sally Willson
March 24, 1815,   William I. Stone and Eliza H. Clayton, Anthony
      Payten, her guardian, gives his consent
March 15, 1815,   Allen McKenny and Alice McKenny
June 19, 1815,   John Power and Elizabeth Reynolds
March 11, 1815,   James Rowles and Nancy Cavender
March 4, 1815,   Meredith Lucas and Jenny Pope
July 3, 1815,   Reuben Jenkins and Rachel Sanders
July 26, 1815,   Reuben Potter and Lucy Fawbush
September 6, 1816,   James Antoney and Fanny Wever
September 24, 1816, F. A. Mungar and Susanna Critcher, John
      Bailey, her guardian, gives his consent
October 28, 1816,   Wm. King and Mary Pillian
January 1, 1816,   Thomas Miller and Jane McNeale
June 28, 1816,   James Sutton and Elizabeth Nelson
September 2, 1816,   William Hall and Sally Coats, Molly Coats,
      her mother, gives her consent
August 31, 1816,   Henry Maskiel and Jane Cary
October 7, 1816,   Samuel Weaver and Martha Gregory
May 22, 1816,   Emanuel Peck and Catharine Peake, Catharine
      Peake, her mother, gives her consent
September 30, 1816,   Pierce Mozingo and Nancy Sutton
April 22, 1816,   George Wilkins and Mary G. Hail
January 15, 1816,   George G. Mothershead and Hannah C. Baber
January 29, 1816,   Henry Mothershead and Sally Weldon
February 6, 1816,   James Edmonds and Margaret Lucas
March 20, 1816,   William King and Sally Robinson, Elizabeth
      Robinson, her mother, gives her consent
February 6, 1816,   Robert Brewer and Sarah Peed
March 11, 1816,   Reuben Briant and Sally Mothershead
January 1, 1816,   John Potter and Polly Butler
May 9, 1816,   William G. Morris and Caty McKenny
March 21, 1816,   Trusel Hall and Isabel Sandy
June 20, 1816,   Owen Sullivan and Nancy Beale
July 6, 1816,   Charles Muir and Margaret Williams
November 2, 1816,   Samuel Davis and Fanny Luttrell
November 9, 1816,   Thornton Nash and Alice Callahan

November 18, 1816, William Kendal and Penelope Bartlett, Elizabeth Bartlett, her mother, gives her consent

December 23, 1816, Thomas Washington and Patsey Teet

December 9, 1816, John S. Head and Lucy Anidel, Mary Anidel,
her mother, gives her consent

December 21, 1816, William Self and Elizabeth Lambert

December 28, 1816, Rodham McCoy and Elizabeth Bruin

December 31, 1816, Thomas Johnson and Ellen Hokkens

May 3, 1816, Whiting Green and Susanah Ryles

August 31, 1816, John Pursley and Elizabeth Carter, John Carter,
her uncle, gives his consent

June 10, 1816, John Washington and Lucy Hinson

September 4, 1816, James W. Nash and Felicia White

February 5, 1816, Ritchie Atkins and Jane Strother

December 23, 1816, Octavious Harvey and Susanna Maria Muse,
Charles Muse, her father, gives his consent

July 25, 1816, Thornton Hinson and Bethiah Sandford

November 8, 1816, Wm. H. McCulloch and Mary W. Douglass,
Jas. Douglass, her father, gives his consent

July 25, 1816, Robert Anton and Elizabeth Howson

July 16, 1816, William L. Rogers and Ann Ballantine Murphy,
Jno. Murphy, her father, gives his consent

June 13, 1816, Bethal Tallant and Nancy Hennage

July 18, 1816, John Pearson and Sarah Nevitt

July 16, 1816, Davie Morgan and Elizabeth B. Lamkin, Bendt
Lamkin, her father, gives his consent

March 20, 1817, Jeremiah Carpenter and Nancy Oliff

May 12, 1817, Thomas Rice and Letty A. Stowers, Thomas
Stowers, her father, gives his consent

March 24, 1817, Henry Lee and Ann R. McCarty

October 7, 1817, John Gibbs and Pinkston C. Askins

December 20, 1817, Nathaniel King and Elizabeth Briscoe

November 6, 1817, Willis Damron and Jemina Rice

February 19, 1817, Thomas A. Publes and Elizabeth Pinkard

June 17, 1817, Thomas Clarke and Eliza Burch

October 17, 1817, Thos. Edwards and Elizabeth S. Templeman

July 14, 1817, Moore F. Brockenbrough and Sarah Ball

September 9, 1817, William Sutton and Trecey M. Sutton

February 15, 1817, Thomas Palmer and Sarah Brown, John Brown,
her father, gives his consent

February 6, 1817, Thomas Mothershead and Fanny Beddo

February 11, 1817,   Silas Short and Jane Sanders
February 15, 1817,   James Brown and Ann Johnson
January 1, 1817,   George F. Tallant and Elizabeth Hinson
November 25, 1817,   James Reamy and Lucy Brewer
June 27, 1817,   Samuel J. Boothe and Mary W. Wright
December 16, 1817,   Thomas Sandy and Alethea Brann
October 30, 1817,   E. Lawson Waring and Eliza Bankhead
January 20, 1817,   Richard Q. Nunn and Catharine Carlton, Lewis
Carlton, her father, gives his consent
July 18, 1817,   James Bland and Sarah Coleman
January 21, 1817,   John Scutt and Fanny Sanford
January 14, 1817,   Robert C. Connollee and Lucy Hazard
January 14, 1817,   Benjamin Jenkins and Susanna Pullen, Catharine Pullen, her mother, gives her consent
January 17, 1817,   John B. Barber and Martha Gawen
January 9, 1817,   Augustus L. Gallagher and Fanny Elmore
January 9, 1817,   James Brann and Susanna Garner
January 7, 1817,   James Jenkins and Frances Bartlett
August 22, 1817,   James Harris and Elizabeth Brown
January 2, 1817,   Levi Briant and Mary Harris
September 10, 1817,   Robert Sandford and Eliza B. Harvey, John
Harvey, her father, gives his consent
December 14, 1818,   William Gawen and Alice Jefferson Garner,
Catharine Garner, her mother, gives her consent
November 30, 1818,   Richard F. Drake and Nancy Edmons
November 30, 1818,   Richard S. Ellis and Emily H. Douglass, Jas.
Douglass, her father, gives his consent
November 19, 1818,   Richard Crask and Frances B. Doleman
January 12, 1818,   Rodham Ashton and Polly Sanford
December 21, 1818,   Aaron Wallace and Elizabeth Brann
January 17, 1818,   John Sanford and Harriot Morrison
March 12, 1818,   Vincent Moore and Polly Wroe
November 23, 1818,   William Sanford and Sarah Hallbrooks
December 18, 1818,   Solomon S. Hutt and Molly P. Redman, Solomon Redman, her guardian, gives his consent
March 11, 1818,   Henry Penn and Elizabeth Johnson
August 27, 1818,   Thomas S. Nash and Pattcy Miller
March 25, 1818,   Robert Sanders and Lusuttah Drake
September 1, 1818,   Ludwell Nash and Mary Sutton
August 31, 1818,   Joshua Reamy and Fanny Morriss
May 27, 1818,   Fleet Lamkin and Elender Chilton

May 5, 1818,	William Short and Alcey Whetley
May 26, 1818,	Spencer Miller and Mahala Morriss
March 9, 1818,	William Johnson and Peggy Smith
March 2, 1818,	Henry Drake and Nancy Reamy
March 12, 1818,	Henry Hungerford and Amelia Spence
February 9, 1818,	Elliott Stone and Ann Clarke
February 13, 1818,	Ebenezer Selvy and Sara Deatley
October 30, 1818,	Patrick S. Sanford and Hannah Butler
January 7, 1818,	Samuel Day and Lotty Ashton

January 20, 1818, Caleb Watts and Margaret Lauder, Jas. Lauder, her father, gives his consent

January 7, 1818,	William Carpenter and Catharine Brewer
January 13, 1818,	James Sanders and Filisha Fisher
December 24, 1817,	Samuel Sutton and Elizabeth Crask
February 13, 1818,	John Carpenter and Nancy Reamy
May 16, 1818,	Peter Lendrum and Elizabeth Askins

May 18, 1818, Robert Murphy and Eliza B. Newton, Sally Newton, her mother, gives her consent

| April 27, 1818, | William Lacy and Nancy Davis |
| March 28, 1818, | William Deatley and Susanner Winstead |

December 21, 1818, Elliott T. Minor and Juliet Underwood, Jno. Underwood, her father, gives his consent

| March 18, 1818, | Elijah Ambrues and Catharine Ollive |
| March 23, 1818, | James Ollive and Susannah Ollive |

December 21, 1818, Downing Cox and Eliza M. Sissin, Charles Muse, her guardian, gives his consent

May 10, 1819,	Lewis Mazard and Frances M. Gilbert
May 4, 1819,	George Reed and Jane Buniff
November 11, 1819,	Thomas Douglass and Nancy S. Johnson
March 17, 1819,	James W. Crask and Elizabeth Bragg
March 30, 1819,	John P. Laycock and Pheby Johnson
February 22, 1819,	James King and Mairy King
May 15, 1819,	Peter Cullison and Meriah Johnson
December 1, 1819,	Richard Weaver and Ann Jenkins
February 6, 1819,	Thos. S. Davers and Mary Elizabeth Field
August 31, 1819,	John Sutton and Martha Stone
December 23, 1819,	Richard Clarke and Elizabeth Hallbrooks

February 19, 1819, Thomas S. Rice and Nancy R. Redman, Solomon Redman

| January 18, 1819, | Fryar Sutton and Elizabeth R. Dozier |
| January 14, 1819, | Daniel Mathaney and Eleanor Beane |

July 30, 1819, William Brinn and Elizabeth Robinson, Hannah
     Robinson, her mother, gives her consent
December 4, 1819,   William S. Bulgar and Mary Basshaw
December 7, 1819,   Campbell Teet and Eliza Pumroy
June 7, 1819,   William H. Sanford and Mary Moxley
June 1, 1819,   William Olliffe and Ann Drake
October 25, 1819, Lawrence Washington and Sarah T. Washing-
     ton, Sarah Washington, her mother, gives her consent
December 23, 1819,   Martin Kilman and Franky Briant
May 25. 1819,   John L. Oliff and Sary Ryals
October 26, 1819,   William Anthony and Susannah McKenney,
     Judah McKenney and Letty McKenney her parents give
     their consent
October 5, 1819, Joseph Winget and Maria Mothershead, Thos.
     Barber, her guardian, gives his consent
September 22, 1819,   William Sanders and Mary Burgess
July 28, 1819,   Henry Bowcock and Catharine Monroe
June 28, 1819,   Ebenezer Morse and Lucindey Carey
February 9, 1819,   Charles Muse and Catharine Jett
January 6, 1819,   Charles Tuxan and Polly Carter
April 26, 1819,   Joseph Gregory and Calvert S. Williams
January 13, 1819,   James Kirk and Sarah Simkins
September 27, 1819,   Meriday Hinson and Hannah Worsencraft
August 23, 1819,   Lofty Olliffe and Susannah Jones
July 26, 1819,   Thomas Newman and Lucy Johnson
April 3, 1819,   Edward Burn and Milly Spurling
May 29, 1819,   Ethelwald Sanford and Salley M. Robinson
January 12, 1819,   Matthew Jenkins and Elizabeth D. Eidson, John
     Eidson, her father, gives his consent
April 1, 1822,   George Jackson and Nancy I. Cole
December 22, 1821,   Francis Lewis and Catharine Smith
November 28, 1822, John Reed and Kitty M. Kelley, James Scates,
     her guardian, gives his consent
May 21, 1822,   William Jackson and Martha Oldham
December 12, 1822,   William Johnson and Elizabeth Mothershead
January 29, 1822,   Benjamin Johnson and Peggy Sandford
June 28, 1822, Fleet Cox and Sarah H. Murphy, John Murphy,
     her father, gives his consent
May 20, 1822,   Jeremiah Lewis and Elizabeth Moore
January 21, 1822,   Henry P. Bowcock and Maria Smith
July 22, 1822,   Josias Clapham and Hannah West Hodge

October 12, 1822,   Henry T. Garnett and Eliza L. Wareing

January 21, 1822,   David Lamb and Ann Bryant

January 9, 1821, Samuel Carpenter and Malinda Spurling, William Spurling, her father, gives his consent

May 27, 1822, William Barnet and Elizabeth Cole, Peggy Cole, her mother, gives her consent

October 16, 1822,   Henry Fauntleroy and Ann L. Sisson

January 21, 1822,   Seth Rockwell and Patty Rust Atwell

June 8, 1822,   John Carroll and Nancy Curtis

June 24, 1822, John P. Newton and Mary E. Cox, Fleet Cox her brother gives his consent.

May 21, 1822,   Jarrot Thompson and Betsy McKoy

July 11, 1822,   Charles Masse and Mary Wilson

May 9, 1822, Robert H. Tapscott and Mary E. Wright, Bendt. Wright, her father, gives his consent

July 11, 1822, Samuel Suite and Elizabeth Marmaduke, Wm. M. Walker, her guardian, gives his consent

December 16, 1822, William Guttridge and Lucy Carpenter, John C. Carpenter her father, gives his consent

April 30, 1821, Henry Waring and Lucy Robb, R. G. Robb her father, gives his consent.

October 18, 1821, George E Roper and Mary Sutton, Frances Sutton, her mother, gives her consent

December 31, 1822,   John Deakins and Elizabeth Teet

December 16, 1822,   John A. Lyell and Sarah A. I. Plummer

October 30, 1822, Daniel Carter and Sally Hinson, M. Hinson, her mother, gives her consent

April 17, 1822, Sylvanus Sampson and Ann Deatley, Christopher Deatley, her father, gives his consent

May 23, 1822, Edward Porter and Mary Montgomery, Andrew Montgomery, her father, gives his consent

January 16, 1822, George Lampkin and Ursley Payne, Ann Payne, her mother, gives her consent

December 26, 1821, James Jones and Sarah Pope, Penelope Pope, her mother, gives her consent

June 6, 1821,   John Randall and Sally Barrott

March 22,1820,   Samuel Mothershead and Elizabeth Dodd

July 17, 1820, James B. Dixon and Elizabeth R. Coghill, Jo. Dixon, his father, gives his consent

July 15, 1820, Edward Inscoe and Jane Winkfield, Edward Winkfield, her father, gives his consent

December 29, 1820,   Matthew Deatley and Mariah Mitchell, Christopher Deatley his father gives his consent

April 10, 1821,   James Pratt and Fanny Jenkins

December 27, 1820,   Richard Mothershead and Mary Stone, William B. Stone, her father, gives his consent

January 10, 1820,   William Brawner and Fanny Nash

November 1, 1820,   Augustine Sanford and Sibbey Mozingo

January 3, 1820,   Richard Edmonds and Penelope Marks

January 1, 1820,   Benjamin Simms and Mary McDaniel

March 22, 1820,   John Sanders and Margaret Tiler

November 27, 1820,   Thomas Martin and Elizabeth C. Payne

February 11, 1820,   George G. Barrok and Mariah James

April 8, 1820,   Meredith Hinson and Hannah Whoosencroft

June 22, 1820,   Thomas S. Muse and Lucinda Harvey

February 16, 1820,   Robert Carter and Margarett Sanders

September 26, 1820,   John Wroe and Mary Bryant

October 5, 1820,   George Wm. Smith and Ann Campbell

March 8, 1820,   John Kirk and Nancy Bedders

May 3, 1820,   Nathaniel Lefever and Winney Short, Clark Short, her father, gives his consent

April 17, 1820,   Charles S. Askins and Nancy Olive

January 11, 1820,   James Guttridge and Susan Hinson, Wm. Hinson, her father, gives his consent

October 16, 1820,   Stephen S. Mothershead and Catharine Sampson

December 27, 1820,   William Brinnon and Elizabeth Cash

December 6, 1820,   Henry A. Riley and Sarah Tiffey

October 18, 1820,   Gerard A. Sanford and Sebina B. Jenkins

May 22, 1820,   John C. Beale and Sally E. Butler

December 20, 1819,   Benjamin Weaver and Alice Weaver

April 3, 1820,   Benedict D. Wright and Sally Smith

September 25, 1820,   Henry Griggs and Lucy Dozier, Rich'd Dozier, her father, gives his consent

November 15, 1820,   George Sisson and Mary Mullins, James Mullins, her father, gives his consent

February 12, 1821,   James Perry and Sally Grinnan, John Grinnan, her father, gives his consent

January 15, 1821,   John Marks and Catharine Kelly

January 2, 1821,   Dozier Garner and Mary Beale

January 22, 1821,   Fleet Damron and Polly Garner

April 23, 1821,   John B. Yeatman and Catharine A. R. J. Maith

July 15, 1821, William Settles and Nancy King, Thos King, her
    father, gives his consent

November 2, 1821, John Morriss and Elizabeth Reamy, Bevinson
    Reamy, her father, gives his consent

October 12, 1821,   William B. Stone and Martha Hall

February 12, 1821,   Nathaniel Green and Elizabeth Jett

August 10, 1821,   Abner James and Lucinda Payton

June 3, 1821,   Silas Short and Catharine Jett

January 31, 1821,   James Rice and Margaret Brown

August 11, 1821, William Redman and Frances Carter, Lettee
    Carter, her mother, gives her consent

August 22, 1821,   Newton Mozingo and Elizabeth Smith

December 24, 1821,   Joel Bartlett and Sally Wilson

January 22, 1821,   Thomas M. Jenkins and Ann P. Hunter

December 31, 1821,   Thomas Nash and Harriott Hinson

December 24, 1821,   John Ramey and Mary McGuire

November 21, 1821, Thomas M. Belfield and Fanny F. Sandford,
    Sibella Sandford, her mother, gives her consent

August 28, 1821,   Youell Davis and Susanna Pecure

April 2, 1821,   Lionel I. Cotterell and Fanny D. Oliff

April 25, 1821,   Solomon Redman and Sally A. Robinson

May 11, 1821,   Trusel B. Hall and Sally Spurling

February 26, 1821,   William K. Morris and Fanny Gutridge

February 17, 1821,   Sidnal Weaver and Elizabeth Harries

February 12, 1821, Lawrence B. Pope and Rocky Grinnan, John
    Grinnan, her father, gives his consent

February 1, 1821, Meredith M. Edwards and Mary B. Canthorn,
    James Mullins, her guardian, gives his consent

June 8, 1821,   John Garner and Elizabeth Brewer

April 3, 1821,   Anderson Sandford and Lucy Clarke

June 9, 1821,   Allen P. Leblanc and Fanny Hilliard

December 26, 1821,   James Ayres and Elizabeth Doleman

March 20, 1821,   William Hennage and Ann N. Hazard

July 12, 1821,   Alexander Dodd and Margaret Griffin

July 3, 1821,   Alexander Weaver and Marthy Alderson

May 14, 1821, Alfred Weaver and Mary Clark, Richard Clark,
    her father, gives his consent

July 10, 1820,   Spencer Miller and Frances James

March 13, 1821, Richard Jackson and Sophia Scates, James Scates,
    her father, gives his consent

February 16, 1821,   Osmond Johnson and Ann H. Crask

October 2, 1821,   John Anthony and Kettnar Thomas
August 20, 1821,   James Davis and Ellen Hall
January 6, 1821,   William C. Chandler and Susan Mongar
January 4, 1821,   Thomas Brewer and Mary Hinson
January 26, 1821,   Youell Teete and Grace Newman
May 3, 1821,   George R. Pitts and C. E. Spence
November 11, 1823,   William Porter and Amanda C. Baber
June 25, 1823,   Jennings A. Yeatman and Caty Sandford
January 23, 1823, George D. Ashton and Catharine Roberta Rose
     Hodge
June 10, 1823,   John H. Peake and Elizabeth Parker
June 16, 1823,   Christopher Talent and Lettice Garner
May 9, 1823,   Christopher Mothershead and Louisa Edmonds
May 29, 1823,   Thomas Gregory and Elizabeth King
July 23, 1823,   Sam'l Coats and Ann Balderson
April 8, 1823,   Wm. Arnold and Mary E. Deatley
April 23, 1823,   John B. Crismond and Sally Ryalls, Charles Cris-
     mond, his father, gives his consent
January 16, 1823, George T. Spilman and Frances Neale, Mary
     Ann Neale, her mother, gives her consent
August 26, 1823,   Peter Smith and Polly Pillman
January 16, 1823,   Thomas Beachan and Betsy Elmore, John
     Elmore, her father, gives his consent
August 28, 1823,   James Nash and Martha Washington
————————1823, John Allen and Fanny Mealey, Daniel Mealey,
     her father, gives his consent
August 10, 1823, Lovell Pierce and Mary Ann Berkley, William
     Berkley, her father, gives his consent
July 8, 1823, Daniel H. Hardwick and Lucy Smith Peter Smith,
     her father, gives his consent
August 10, 1823,   Catesby Collinsworth and Mary Tiffey
December 29, 1823,   Thomas Lamkin and Elizabeth B. Morgan
December 29, 1823,   Gerard McKenney and Polly Christopher
     Lewis, Edward D. Lewis, her father, gives his consent
December 29, 1823,   Albert J. Reamy and Mahala M. Mathes,
     Pripey Mathes, her father, gives his consent
December 10, 1823,   Benjamin R. Head and Ann Jett
January 3, 1823,   Edward Laycock and Polly B. Wilkins
February 18, 1823, James L. Monroe and Rachel C. Smith, Wm.
     W. Smith, her father, gives his consent

November 10, 1823, Wm. Cridlin and Alcey Reade, Nelson Crid-
lin, his father, gives his consent
February 20, 1823,   Richard Miller and Adelaide T. Reaniy
Marcn 19, 1823,   Henry Parker and Elizabeth Downing
————1823,   Michael Orsboun and Charlotte Clark
December 31, 1822,   Thomas E. D. Combs and Ann Dodd
December 25, 1822, John T. Smith and Mary M. Smith, William
W. Smith, her father, gives his consent
January 29, 1823, Austin Wilkerson and Susanna A. Brinnon, Jos
Wilkerson, his guardian, gives his consent
November 20, 1823, Charles Lewis and Ann Head, Rachel Head,
her mother, gives her consent
December 29, 1823,   William L. Beale and Frances G. Garner
January 8, 1823,   James T. Furgusson and Fanny Davis
January 7, 1823,   Ishmael Bragg and Mary Dozier
January 14, 1823,   James Collins and Prissillia McCay
January 14, 1823,   Blanc Ashton and Susan Sorrel
January 4, 1823,   John Roe and Elizabeth Coats
January 7, 1824, Richard McKenney and Alice B. Potter, Nancy
Potter, her mother, gives her consent.
July 31, 1824,   John S. Carter and Ann Pierce
April 13, 1824, Griffin T. King and Ann H. English, James Eng-
lish, her father, gives his consent
January 21, 1824,   Presley Weaver and Mary Alverson
January 20, 1824,   William Carpenter and Mary Pope
January 6, 1824, William G. Kirk and Mary Whealler, Richard
Whealler, her father, gives his consent
January 14, 1824,   Meredith Deatley and Lucinda Weaver
January 10, 1824, Thomas Anadale and Ann C. Poor, Thomas
Poor, her father, gives his consent
January 19, 1824, William H. Sisson and Susanna W. Sandford,
Edward Sandford, her father, gives his consent
July 20, 1824,   Samuel Anton and Susanna Gregory
November 30, 1824,   James Grisset and Jane Winkfield
July 28, 1824,   Christopher Brown and Nancy Foxhall
February 2, 1824, James R. Low and Fanny Gregory, Thos. Gre-
gory, her father, gives his consent
February 3, 1824,   Jeremiah Smith and Fanny Sutton
February 19, 1824,   Wm. Tallent and Lucy Davis
February 18, 1824,   Henry Weaver and Ann Omohundro
February 21, 1824,   Thos. Pilsbury and Maria Hall

December 20, 1824, Rodaham Sanford and Minerva J. Mothershead, Jane Mothershead, her mother, gives her consent

December 9, 1824,   John Bragg and Caty Garner

September 7, 1824,   Wm. D. Robinson and Sarah Richardia Cox

October 19, 1824,   Thomas Jones and Polly Tete

January 22, 1824,   James Morse and Frances Crabb

January 22, 1824,   William King and Mary Damurn

December 27, 1824, Wm. Tete and Sintha Tete, James Tete, her father, gives his consent

April 12, 1824,   Edward Porter and Elizabeth Tiffey

April 26, 1824,   George B. Danks and Mary Cane

July 28, 1824, Henry Eliff and Frances Stone, Alice Stone, her mother, gives her consent

July 7, 1824,   Robert McKoy and Judith Day

November 26, 1824, Peter Claughton and Hannah R. Lamkin, Bendt. Lamkin, her father, gives his consent

December 23, 1824,   Richard Coleman and Mary Moore

June 28, 1824, William Payton and Codelia Bruce, Richard Bayne, her guardian, gives his consent

December 23, 1824,   Thomas Omohundro and Sary P. Hunter

January 21, 1824, James Morriss and Sophia Dodd, James S. Mothershead, her guardian, gives his consent

July 21, 1824,   Fennor Hinson and Rebeckah Carpenter

November 9, 1824,   Simon Read and Frankey Weldon

June 11, 1824, Hiram Smither and Sally Carter, Sally Carter, her mother, gives her consent

INDEX

Woodcock 39
Woodridge 69
Woodroof 34
Woods 87
Woodson 39, 50, 71
Woollard 94
Woosencroft 106, 109
Wormeley 52, 56, 75,
  77, 79, 80
Wormley 57
Worsencraft 130
Worsham 70, 72
Worth 100, 115
Wortham 76, 77, 78, 79
Wren 19
Wright 9, 10, 16, 17, 27,
  37, 44, 45, 47, 72, 92,
  100, 101, 116, 119,
  123, 128, 131, 132

Wroe 95, 105, 107, 108,
  110, 128, 132
Wyatt 37, 41, 68, 80
Wyche 29, 30, 34
Wynn 67
Wynne 44, 45
Wythe 81, 82

Yancy 41
Yarborough 62
Yardley 110, 120, 125
Yarrington 76
Yates 74, 79, 80
Yeatman 93, 97, 100,
  104, 108, 110, 116,
  119, 122, 132, 134
Yeo 82
Yerby 48, 52, 53, 54,
  56

Young 10, 17, 23, 24,
  33, 39, 82, 85, 87, 95,
  107
Younglove 19

Zells 32
Zolle 23

www.ingramcontent.com/pod-product-compliance
Lightning Source LLC
Chambersburg PA
CBHW061744270326
41928CB00011B/2373